MW01115376

including
- *Life of Shakespeare*
- *Background of* Henry V
- *Genealogical Tables*
- *Plot Summary of* Henry V
- *List of Characters*
- *Summaries and Commentaries*
- *Sixteenth-Century Political Theory*
- *Questions for Review*
- *Selected Bibliography*

by
Jeffery Fisher, M.F.A.
University of Tennessee

INCORPORATED

LINCOLN, NEBRASKA   68501

Editor	Consulting Editor
Gary Carey, M.A.	*James L. Roberts, Ph.D.*
University of Colorado	*Department of English*
	University of Nebraska

ISBN 0-8220-0029-6

© Copyright 1981

by

Cliffs Notes, Inc.

All Rights Reserved

Printed in U.S.A.

1996 Printing

The Cliffs Notes logo, the names "Cliffs" and "Cliffs Notes," and the black and yellow diagonal-stripe cover design are all registered trademarks belonging to Cliffs Notes, Inc., and may not be used in whole or in part without written permission.

Cliffs Notes, Inc.   Lincoln, Nebraska

CONTENTS

HENRY V NOTES

LIFE OF SHAKESPEARE

Many books have assembled facts, reasonable suppositions, traditions, and speculations concerning the life and career of William Shakespeare. Taken as a whole, these materials give a rather comprehensive picture of England's foremost dramatic poet. Tradition and sober supposition are not necessarily false because they lack proved bases for their existence. It is important, however, that persons interested in Shakespeare should distinguish between *facts* and *beliefs* about his life.

From one point of view, modern scholars are fortunate to know as much as they do about a man of middle-class origin who left a small English country town and embarked on a professional career in sixteenth-century London. From another point of view, they know surprisingly little about the writer who has continued to influence the English language and its drama and poetry for more than three hundred years. Sparse and scattered as these facts of his life are, they are sufficient to prove that a man from Stratford by the name of William Shakespeare wrote the major portion of the thirty-seven plays which scholars ascribe to him. The concise review which follows will concern itself with some of these records.

No one knows the exact date of William Shakespeare's birth. His baptism occurred on Wednesday, April 26, 1564. His father was John Shakespeare, tanner, glover, dealer in grain, and town official of Stratford; his mother, Mary, was the daughter of Robert Arden, a prosperous gentleman-farmer. The Shakespeares lived on Henley Street.

Under a bond dated November 28, 1582, William Shakespeare and Anne Hathaway entered into a marriage contract. The baptism of their eldest child, Susanna, took place in Stratford in May, 1583. One year and nine months later their twins, Hamnet and Judith, were christened in the same church. The parents named them for the poet's friends Hamnet and Judith Sadler.

Early in 1596, William Shakespeare, in his father's name, applied to the College of Heralds for a coat of arms. Although positive proof is lacking, there is reason to believe that the Heralds granted this request, for in 1599 Shakespeare again made application for the right to quarter his coat of arms with that of his mother. Entitled to her father's coat of arms, Mary had lost this privilege when she married John Shakespeare before he held the official status of gentleman.

In May of 1597, Shakespeare purchased New Place, the outstanding residential property in Stratford at that time. Since John Shakespeare had suffered financial reverses prior to this date, William must have achieved success for himself.

Court records show that in 1601 or 1602, William Shakespeare began rooming in the household of Christopher Mountjoy in London. Subsequent disputes between Shakespeare's landlord, Mountjoy, and his son-in-law, Stephen Belott, over Stephen's wedding settlement led to a series of legal actions, and in 1612 the court scribe recorded Shakespeare's deposition of testimony relating to the case.

In July, 1605, William Shakespeare paid four hundred and forty pounds for the lease of a large portion of the tithes on certain real estate in and near Stratford. This was an arrangement whereby Shakespeare purchased half the annual tithes, or taxes, on certain agricultural products from sections of land in and near Stratford. In addition to receiving approximately ten percent income on his investment, he almost doubled his capital. This was possibly the most important and successful investment of his lifetime, and it paid a steady income for many years.

Shakespeare is next mentioned when John Combe, a resident of Stratford, died on July 12, 1614. To his friend, Combe bequeathed the sum of five pounds. These records and similar ones are important, not because of their economic significance but because they prove the existence of a William Shakespeare in Stratford and in London during this period.

On March 25, 1616, William Shakespeare revised his last will and testament. He died on April 23 of the same year. His body lies within the chancel and before the altar of the Stratford church. A rather wry inscription is carved upon his tombstone:

Good Friend, for Jesus' sake, forbear
To dig the dust enclosed here;
Blest be the man that spares these stones
And curst be he that moves my bones.

The last direct descendant of William Shakespeare was his grand-daughter, Elizabeth Hall, who died in 1670.

These are the most outstanding facts about Shakespeare the man, as apart from those about the dramatist and poet. Such pieces of information, scattered from 1564 through 1616, declare the existence of such a person, not as a writer or actor, but as a private citizen. It is illogical to think that anyone would or could have fabricated these details for the purpose of deceiving later generations.

In similar fashion, the evidence establishing William Shakespeare as the foremost playwright of his day is positive and persuasive. Robert Greene's *Groatsworth of Wit*, in which he attacked Shakespeare, a mere actor, for presuming to write plays in competition with Greene and his fellow playwrights, was entered in the *Stationers' Register* on September 20, 1592. In 1594 Shakespeare acted before Queen Elizabeth, and in 1594 and 1595 his name appeared as one of the shareholders of the Lord Chamberlain's Company. Francis Meres in his *Palladis Tamia* (1598) called Shakespeare "mellifluous and hony-tongued" and compared his comedies and tragedies with those of Plautus and Seneca in excellence.

Shakespeare's continued association with Burbage's company is equally definite. His name appears as one of the owners of the Globe in 1599. On May 19, 1603, he and his fellow actors received a patent from James I designating them as the King's Men and making them Grooms of the Chamber. Late in 1608 or early in 1609, Shakespeare and his colleagues purchased the Blackfriars Theatre and began using it as their winter location when weather made production at the Globe inconvenient.

Other specific allusions to Shakespeare, to his acting and his writing, occur in numerous places. Put together, they form irrefutable testimony that William Shakespeare of Stratford and London was the leader among Elizabethan playwrights.

One of the most impressive of all proofs of Shakespeare's authorship of his plays is the First Folio of 1623, with the dedicatory verse which appeared in it. John Heminge and Henry Condell, members of Shakespeare's own company, stated that they collected and issued the plays as a memorial to their fellow actor. Many contemporary poets contributed eulogies to Shakespeare; one of the best known of these poems is by Ben Jonson, a fellow actor and, later, a friendly rival. Jonson also criticized Shakespeare's dramatic work in *Timber: or, Discoveries* (1641).

Certainly there are many things about Shakespeare's genius and career which the most diligent scholars do not know and cannot explain, but the facts which do exist are sufficient to establish Shakespeare's identity as a man and his authorship of the thirty-seven plays which reputable critics acknowledge to be his.

THE BACKGROUND OF *HENRY V*

Since *Henry V* is the last play of Shakespeare's tetralogy, the earlier three plays shed some light upon the present play. The Elizabethan audiences which Shakespeare was writing for would have known these earlier plays and, of course, they would have been familiar with many of the characters in this play. Therefore, since *Henry V* is the play which shows King Henry V as the ideal Christian monarch, the earlier plays leading up to this figure of perfection are enlightening. For example, when Henry prays just before the Battle of Agincourt, he says:

> Not to-day, O Lord,
> O, not to-day, think not upon the fault
> My father made in compassing the crown.
> (IV.i.310-12)

He is referring to the manner in which his father, Henry IV, became king. The *fault* referred to is the deposition and murder of Richard II, a theme which runs throughout all of the plays in this tetralogy. Henry V, therefore, is the Christian king who wears a crown gotten by questionable means. Furthermore, characters like Bardolph and

Pistol and Hostess Quickly had appeared in some of these earlier plays, and there are many references to the famous Sir John Falstaff, one of Shakespeare's greatest comic creations. Therefore, a brief knowledge of the earlier plays will clearly enhance the reading, enjoyment, and understanding of *Henry V.*

RICHARD II (Synopsis)

The play opens with a dispute between Henry Bolingbroke, Duke of Hereford, and Thomas Mowbray, Duke of Norfolk. Bolingbroke has accused Mowbray of treason, and the two of them exchange insults in the presence of King Richard. After attempts to reconcile them fail, Richard orders them to take part in a traditional chivalric trial by combat. On the field of combat, the king changes his mind and banishes the two men—Bolingbroke for ten years (commuted to six) and Mowbray for life. Then the king makes plans to leave for the wars in Ireland.

Before departing, Richard visits the ailing father of Bolingbroke, John of Gaunt, Duke of Lancaster. Gaunt warns Richard with his dying words that he is flirting with danger and doing great harm to the country by allowing himself to be influenced by his sycophantic courtiers. When the old man dies, Richard takes possession of all of Gaunt's wealth and sets out for Ireland.

Unhappy with Richard's incompetence as a ruler and worried by his seizure of the Duke of Lancaster's wealth, a number of nobles rally support for Henry Bolingbroke. When Bolingbroke and his army decide to return from exile in France, the rebel forces prepare to confront Richard on his return from Ireland.

The rebel noblemen force the king to abdicate, and Bolingbroke is crowned as Henry IV. Richard is imprisoned in Pomfret Castle, where he faces his death alone, philosophically contemplating the meaning of his fall from grandeur. Sir Pierce of Exton decides solely on his own to execute the deposed king; as a result, he is banished by King Henry. The play ends with Henry IV planning a penitential pilgrimage to the Holy Land.

HENRY IV, PART I (Synopsis)

When the play opens, King Henry has called the Percies—Northumberland, Worcester, and Hotspur—to the palace. He demands to know why the ranking Scottish prisoners taken by Hotspur have not been turned over to him. The Percies are furious with Henry's seeming arrogance; they deeply resent the fact that this man whom they helped to the throne should demand absolute obedience from them. Thus, they begin to plot their revolt.

Meanwhile, in the comic subplot, Prince Hal and his boon companions make plans to rob a group of travelers in order to play a practical joke on their beloved, blustering cohort, Sir John Falstaff. The joke almost backfires, but Falstaff manages to barely escape and back at the tavern, he emerges triumphantly as the comic hero of the escapade. The merrymaking is interrupted, however, when Prince Hal is called back to court on urgent business.

Hotspur's threats were serious; meeting with Worcester, Mortimer, and Glendower at the residence of the Archdeacon in North Wales, the men plan a campaign against the royal forces; afterward, they plan to divide England into three parts. Momentarily, Hotspur is dejected that he cannot count on Northumberland's troops, but he reasons that perhaps the populace will be even more impressed when they realize that Hotspur accomplished his *coup* without Northumberland's help.

When he learns that Henry's royal army has set forth for battle, Hotspur is again worried—this time about the news that Prince Hal accompanies his father's troops as second in command. But deciding that his victory will seem even more miraculous if he can dispose of Hal personally, Hotspur vows to kill Hal himself, and his ardor and impetuosity is rekindled.

When the plot returns to the comic characters, Falstaff is arrayed as a military commander, leading a group of pitiful, physically unfit "soldiers" who vow they will fight for England. Both Prince Hal and Westmoreland remark on the company's unfitness, but they decide to let them continue to march. In the meantime, the Archbishop of York is alarmed to learn of the Percies' plot and about the fact that neither Mortimer nor Northumberland will be accompanying Hotspur's men; he fears reprisal from King Henry if Hotspur is defeated.

In parley at the king's camp at Shrewsbury with two of Hotspur's allies, Worcester and Vernon, Prince Hal speaks words of praise for Hotspur, modestly concedes that he himself has been derelict, and he offers to fight his rival in single combat, in place of an all-out battle between the two opposing forces. The two rebel leaders depart, ostensibly to report to Hotspur what has been said by the king and the prince.

Hotspur impatiently decides to engage in total combat. During the course of the battle, most of Falstaff's men are killed; Hal heroically rescues his father from the sword of Douglas, a Scottish Earl; and he slays his rival, Hotspur. Worcester and Vernon are captured and later put to death, but Douglas is released by a generous Prince Hal. The rebel forces have been badly defeated, and King Henry sends another of his sons, John of Lancaster, to the North, where John will oppose Northumberland and Archbishop Scroop; Henry himself will leave with Prince Hal to fight the forces led by Glendower and Mortimer.

HENRY IV, PART II (Synopsis)

When Part I closed, Henry IV was dispatching his son John of Lancaster to the north to fight Northumberland and Archbishop Scroop; this play now opens with Northumberland receiving conflicting news about the results of the Battle of Shrewsbury. When he hears of the defeat and death of his son Hotspur, he flees to Scotland to await further developments. Meanwhile, Falstaff becomes involved with Mistress Quickly, and he uses his royal commission to avoid being imprisoned for debt. He continues his riotous feasting and drinking and joking with Prince Hal. Prince Hal, however, while tolerating the unrestrained behavior of Falstaff, nevertheless shows some concern for his royal father and for the affairs of the realm. Since the prince has already shown his valor and honor at the Battle of Shrewsbury, we are now more receptive to his comic behavior with Falstaff, as he once more endorses the precept that life should have its lighter moments—as we will see in *Henry V*, when King Henry plays a practical joke on Williams, a common soldier.

Meanwhile, Prince John moves against the rebel forces and is able to subdue them and arrest the leaders for high treason. This news, however, does not gladden the dying King Henry IV because his main concern is with the conduct of Prince Hal, who at this moment is dining with Poins and other lowly associates. Henry ponders the fate of England when Prince Hal becomes king, and he hopes, above all, for unity among his sons. Prince Hal is defended by the Earl of Warwick, who argues that the prince is schooling himself to understand even the lowliest subject, and he predicts that Prince Hal will turn "past evils to advantage."

Prince Hal enters at this point and learns that his father is gravely ill. Everyone leaves except the heir-apparent, who says that he will keep watch at his father's bedside. Observing his father's crown, he philosophizes about it as a symbol of care and anxiety. Noticing his father in a stupor, he concludes that he is dead, and he lifts the crown and places it on his head, reflecting still further about the responsibilities that the crown encompasses. After he leaves the room, the king awakens, sees the crown on his son's head, and immediately assumes that Prince Hal is anxious to see him dead. In a touching speech, he speaks to Prince Hal and reproves him for being impatient to wear the crown; he accuses the prince of having no love for his father and laments that the prince's years of unruly behavior have culminated in such a conclusion.

Prince Hal convincingly asserts his love and respect for his father; he says that he wishes him to live for a long time yet. Obviously affected by Prince Hal's love for him, the king admits that he came to the throne by "bypaths and crooked ways," and he implores God to forgive him for deposing an anointed ruler (Richard II). Prince Hal promises that he will defend the crown against all the world.

For some time, everyone has expected total misrule and chaos when Prince Hal would finally become King Henry V. Especially concerned has been the Lord Chief Justice of England, who had, only a short time before, banished Falstaff and, upon the late king's order, briefly imprisoned the prince. Contrary to all expectations, Henry V approves of all of the actions of the Lord Chief Justice and bids him to continue to serve the crown in his present capacity. The new king then assures his brothers that his life of wild living ended with his father's death, and he is now a completely reformed prince. To the surprise of all present, the king begins to personify immense magnanimity and dedication to duty. It is to be recalled from the very beginning of the two-part chronicle history that Shakespeare has prepared the way for this important order and justice; at last, in *Henry V*, Henry becomes the ideal Christian ruler.

With the ascension of Prince Hal to the throne, Falstaff immediately envisions all types of grand rewards for himself, and he also expects high honors for Hal's other comrades from the tavern. Expecting to reap extravagant benefits, Falstaff immediately leaves for the coronation. When Falstaff approaches the king, however, Henry orders the Lord Chief Justice to reprove the old fellow. Falstaff is incredulous and addresses Henry directly, calling "My King! My Jove! I speak to thee, my heart!" In chilling words, Henry answers, "I know thee not, old man." He then lectures Falstaff about his lifestyle, admonishing him to reform, and if amends are made, then Falstaff can return by slow degrees to the king's favor.

Everyone is amazed and all approve of Henry's actions. At the close of the play, we learn that Henry has called for the assembly of Parliament and that he will soon lead an invasion into France to claim it for England, as we will see in the first act of *Henry V*.

GENEALOGICAL TABLES

The following tables chart the descendants of Edward III, whose grandson Richard II was the last of the Plantagenet line of kings. Reference is made by the Duchess of Gloucester in *Richard II* (I.ii.11) to Edward's seven sons. Of these, only four had descendants who figured later in contests for the throne, forming two new lines of kings, the Lancastrian and the Yorkist, contending with varying success in the Wars of the Roses until Richard III was killed in the battle of Bosworth in 1485 and his niece Elizabeth of York married the Lancastrian heir Henry Tudor, founding the Tudor line. Names of kings are in capitals; "m." indicates "married."

EDWARD III, reigned from 1327 to 1377

Edward, the Black Prince	William of Hatfield	Lionel of Clarence	John of Gaunt	Edmund of York	William of Windsor	Thomas, Duke of Gloucester

Edward, the Black Prince
m. Joan Plantagenet; by 1st husband Thomas Holland

RICHARD II   Thomas, Earl of Huntingdon
m. (1) Anne of Bohemia
   (2) Isabella of France   Duke of Surrey   Joan Holland,
                                                 Duchess of
                                                 York

Hence we learn that the Earl of Surrey and the Duchess of York were step-nephew and step-niece of Richard II

Lionel of Clarence

Philippa m. Edward
                Mortimer

Roger, Earl of March

Edmund, Earl of March

Lionel, the 3rd son had only a daughter ineligible for the throne, but her grandson Edmund Mortimer, Earl of March, lays claim to it in the rebellion under Henry IV.

14

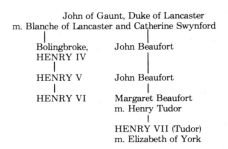

John of Gaunt, Duke of Lancaster
m. Blanche of Lancaster and Catherine Swynford

Bolingbroke, HENRY IV	John Beaufort
HENRY V	John Beaufort
HENRY VI	Margaret Beaufort m. Henry Tudor
	HENRY VII (Tudor) m. Elizabeth of York

The Lancastrian kings were Henry IV, 1399-1413, Henry V, 1413-22, and Henry VI, 1422-71.

Henry VI's incompetence led to Wars of the Roses, the murder of Henry in 1471, and seizure of the throne by the Yorkist Edward IV.

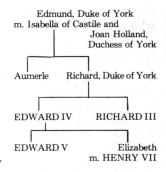

Edmund, Duke of York
m. Isabella of Castile and
Joan Holland,
Duchess of York

Aumerle	Richard, Duke of York
EDWARD IV	RICHARD III
EDWARD V	Elizabeth m. HENRY VII

The Yorkist kings were Edward IV, 1471-83, Edward V, 1483-83, and Richard III, 1483-85. Richard murdered his nephew Edward V and seized the throne.

In 1485, Henry Tudor, the great-great-great grandson of Edward III and leader of the Lancastrian line, ended the Wars of the Roses by killing Richard in the Battle of Bosworth. To unite the Lancastrians and Yorkists, he married Elizabeth, the Yorkist heiress and the great-great granddaughter of Edward III.

Thus was founded the House of Tudor, of which Elizabeth was the reigning queen during most of the life of Shakespeare. His purpose in writing the plays of the Henrys, *Henry IV, Parts I* and *II*, *Henry V*, and *Henry VI, Parts I, II*, and *III*, was to glorify the monarchy of England and instruct the nation in patriotism and in pride of their political institutions.

GENERAL PLOT SUMMARY OF *HENRY V*

As indicated at the close of *Henry IV, Part II*, King Henry V is planning on entering into a war with France over some disputed lands and titles. He has instructed the Archbishop to be sure that his claims are valid. When the play opens, the Archbishop explains to his Bishop how he plans to convince the king to enter into a war with France, thus protecting the church's property, which might otherwise be placed in the hands of the state rather than left it in the church's control.

After the king is convinced of the validity of his claims, an ambassador from France arrives with a rejection of the claims; he also delivers an insulting barrel of tennis balls from the French Dauphin, who still considers King Henry to be the silly and rowdy Prince Hal.

As they are on the verge of leaving for France, King Henry is tending to some business—releasing a prisoner for a minor offense—and then he turns to three of his trusted advisors and has then executed for conspiring with the French to assassinate him. Meanwhile, in the French court, no one seems to take Henry seriously. The entire court is contemptuous of his claims and of his abilities. They are so overconfident that they do not send help to the town of Harfleur, which Henry easily conquers. After this victory, Henry gives strict instructions that all the citizens are to be treated with mercy and that his soldiers are not to loot, rob, or insult the native population. However, a companion from Hal's youth, Bardolph, an inveterate thief, steals a small communion plate, and, as a result, he is executed.

In spite of the English victory, the French still do not express concern, even though the Princess Katharine is involved; if Henry is victorious, she will become the Queen of England; as a result, she feels the necessity to learn the English language, and so she begins taking instructions in that language. Meanwhile, the reports that the English are sick and tattered allow the French to prepare for the battle with complete confidence, especially since they outnumber the English 60,000 to 12,000 troops.

Just before the crucial Battle of Agincourt, an emissary once again approaches King Henry with demands that he immediately surrender his person. His demands are rejected, and King Henry, in a patriotic speech, urges his troops to fight for "Harry, England, and St. George." By miraculous means, the English are victorious and the French are shamed into submission. At the end of the play, King Henry's demands are granted, and he is seen wooing and winning Princess Katharine as his future queen.

LIST OF CHARACTERS

THE ENGLISH

King Henry V

The ruling monarch, who is presented in the play as the ideal Christian king. The main purpose of the play is to convey the idea that Henry V represents in all aspects the model of the ideal ruler. (For a summation of Henry's character, see pp. 69-72).

The Duke of Exeter

He is the uncle of Henry V and a trusted advisor; he functions as both a statesman and as a warrior. Even though he is left in charge of the city of Harfleur, where he is instructed to rule with leniency, he turns up at the Battle of Agincourt, and later he acts as the English ambassador and mediator of the treaty between Henry V and the King of France.

The Duke of Bedford

A brother to Henry, he is used to suggest the close familial bonds between the two brothers. (Historically, he was not present at the Battle of Agincourt, since Henry had appointed him as Regent of England during his absence in France.)

The Duke of Gloucester

Henry's youngest brother. Although he is present in most of the scenes where Henry appears, he has little function in the drama except to illustrate, as Bedford does, familial loyalty. He is placed in charge of some military operations, and he is gently chided by his brother Henry for hoping that the French will not attack while the army is tired. His remark allows Henry to speak on the necessity of relying on the Divine Providence of God: "We are in God's hand, brother, not in theirs."

The Duke of York

Henry's cousin, whom he is very fond of; upon learning of his death during the Battle of Agincourt, Henry is moved to tears when he hears of the duke's courage and his last words of loyalty to the king.

The Archbishop of Canterbury

He is a man of great learning and a master of the English language. He is one of the first persons who brings forth Henry's claim to the French lands, and by so doing, he protects the church's own property from being taken for royal expenditures. He is an extremely astute man, supporting Henry's army with heavy levies from the church; because of this, he is able to retain for the church the basic lands from which the levies are derived.

The Bishop of Ely

An assistant to the Archbishop, he functions mainly as a sounding board for the Archbishop's ideas.

The Earl of Cambridge, Lord Scroop, and Sir Thomas Grey

The conspirators who accept money from France to assassinate Henry V. They are discovered and immediately executed for treason. Their betrayal of Henry evokes from the king a bitter denunciation of their intentions and causes him to wonder whom he can trust. Lord Scroop and the Earl of Cambridge had been especially good friends and confidants of the king.

The Earl of Westmoreland

Another of Henry's administrators who, early in the play, urges him to press for his claims in France.

The Earl of Salisbury

His only function in the drama is to give a patriotic speech in Act IV, when it is discovered that the French armies far outnumber the English forces. He gives a six-line speech and is heard of no more.

The Earl of Warwick

Like the Earl of Salisbury, he plays no particular role in the drama. He appears in several scenes, but speaks only one line in the entire play. He is sent along with Gloucester to make sure that Fluellen and Williams do not get into a real fight; otherwise, he has no function.

18

Captain Fluellen

An intensely loyal Welshman who provides much of the humor in the play by his eagerness to argue and to show off his knowledge of the classics, even though he gets most things mixed up. He is a very proud, opinionated, conceited, testy person who is willing to argue with anyone about anything.

Captain Gower

A friend of Fluellen's, he often serves merely to draw out Fluellen's eccentricities. He is a good soldier who is actually more perceptive about human nature than is Fluellen, and he realizes quickly that Pistol is a cowardly braggart.

Captain Jamy

A Scotsman who appears only briefly in Act III, Scene 2, and seems to immensely enjoy arguing.

Captain Macmorris

He appears only in Act III, Scene 2, when he gets into an argument with Fluellen concerning the Irish.

Bardolph

This character is retained from the earlier *Henry IV* plays, where he was distinguished by having a bad complexion, a fiery red nose, and carbuncles on his cheeks. For some reason, he is now a lieutenant in this play, but he is still a coward and a thief. He is hanged during the course of the play for stealing a communion plate from a French church.

Pistol

Like Bardolph, Pistol also appears in the *Henry IV* plays and thus would be a character that the audience would be familiar with. He is a ranting and raving coward, a "swaggering rascal," a "fustian rascal," and a "bottle-ale rascal." At the end of Act V, Scene 1, Pistol is finally dispensed with, thus bringing to a close a series of characters that began three plays earlier in *Henry IV, Part I.*

Nym

A corporal who is as much of a coward as Bardolph and Pistol are, and he is also an accomplice in their thefts. Like Bardolph, Nym ends up on the gallows.

The Boy

One of Shakespeare's magnificent minor characters, he is younger than the others, and yet he has the quick wit and intelligence to discern the cowardice of Bardolph, Nym, and Pistol. When they try to teach him how to pick pockets, he is outraged and threatens to leave their service. Unfortunately, he is killed when the French raid King Henry's supply area during the Battle of Agincourt.

Hostess Quickly

A simple, uneducated woman who is married to Pistol, but has an unabashed admiration for Sir John Falstaff. She dies of the French malady (syphilis) just before Pistol is to return to England.

Michael Williams

One of the three soldiers whom King Henry, in disguise, meets the night before the Battle of Agincourt. He questions the king's rightness to wage this war, but he never questions his own obedience to the crown. He wonders if the king doesn't have a heavy moral obligation for the souls of those who die in battle. Williams even wonders if the king could not use himself for ransom so that the rest of them will not get killed. When Henry, in disguise, challenges Williams, Williams accepts and they promise to fight each other if they are both alive after the Battle of Agincourt. They exchange gloves so as to recognize each other. Afterwards, when it is discovered that he was arguing and challenging the king, Williams defends himself in such an honest and straightforward manner that the king rewards him with a glove filled with money.

John Bates and Alexander Court

Along with Williams, these two men represent the average or common English soldier. Court has only one line, but Bates has a slightly larger role; for example, he does not share Williams's concern as to whether or not the king's cause is a just one; it is sufficient enough for him to know his duty, and his duty is to fight for the king.

THE FRENCH

Charles VI

The quiet and dignified King of France, who is able to sense the impending danger caused by the approaching English forces, but whereas he grasps the significance, he cannot communicate his fears to the French nobility. He orders his son, the Dauphin, not to go to battle, but apparently this order is ignored since the Dauphin is at the Battle of Agincourt. In the final scene of the play, Charles delivers a gentle speech which is conciliatory as he looks forward to a time of peace and a prosperous union with England through the son whom he hopes his daughter Kate will provide King Henry.

The Dauphin

Next in line for the throne of France, the Dauphin is insolent, opinionated, and stubborn. He knows of Henry's wild, youthful escapades, but he is not perceptive enough to realize that Henry has changed. He still thinks of Henry as a mere wastrel, a young man to whom no attention should be paid. Therefore, he sends Henry a barrel of tennis balls, implying that Henry should content himself with playing ball and not waging war. At the Battle of Agincourt, the Dauphin is more concerned with singing the praises of his horse than he is with the serious business of war. After the defeat of the French, he bitterly feels the shame of it, and he does not appear again in the play.

The Constable of France

The official commander-in-chief of the French forces, he stands out as one of the most capable of the French forces. Yet ultimately, he too succumbs to the temptation of not taking the English seriously; as a result, he is soundly beaten by them.

The Duke of Burgundy

One of the powerful French noblemen and one of the officials of the court, he is responsible for drafting the treaty at the end of the play; he delivers a splendid speech on the virtues of peace.

The Duke of Orleans

Like the other French lords, he is boastful and contemptuous of the English forces, but he does defend the Dauphin when the Constable suggests that the Dauphin might not be as brave as he would like people to believe.

The Duke of Bourbon

One of the French lords who is terribly ashamed about the "ready losses" of the French to the English: "Shame and eternal shame, nothing but shame."

Montjoy

The French herald, or messenger, in charge of delivering the various ultimatums from the French to the English. After the defeat of the French, he comes humbly to ask for peace and request permission for the French to be allowed to collect their dead.

Rambures and Grandpré

Two French lords who appear only briefly.

The Duke of Bretagne and The Duke of Berri

Two noblemen who are onstage only briefly and receive orders from the King of France.

Queen Isabel

The French queen who joins in the negotiations for peace in the hope that her feminine voice will help soothe certain matters in the negotiations. She is pleased with the union between Henry and her daughter Kate and hopes for a strong union of the two kingdoms as a result of the marriage.

Katharine

A young girl of fourteen who accepts the fact that she will be given to Henry as his bride; consequently, she is beginning to learn English for that day when she will be Queen of England.

Alice

Katharine's lady-in-waiting; she is the well-mannered companion of the young princess.

SUMMARIES AND COMMENTARIES

ACT I—PROLOGUE

Summary

The Chorus (one person) enters and calls upon the "Muse" to help in presenting this play since it deals with such a lofty subject matter. The Chorus explains that the small Elizabethan stage can hardly transform itself into the fields of France, or into an English court, or into a battlefield upon which thousands of horses and soldiers fight; with imagination, however, when "we talk of horses . . . you [can] see them" moving across the landscape. Thus the greatness of the subject matter—a subject dealing with England's ideal king, Henry V—requires that the audience exert its greatest imagination to be able to see in their minds the vastness and the splendor that the play recalls. The audience must also be tolerant of the actors who attempt to portray personages of such high estate. And finally, the audience must be prepared for "jumping o'er times" back and forth, from England to France.

Commentary

Because of the ambitions of the playwright and the limitations of the Elizabethan stage, an introduction is in order and the Prologue serves as that introduction. Chronologically, this is only the second time in Shakespeare's career that he has used the device of a Chorus to introduce a drama (the first time he used a Chorus, it introduced *Romeo and Juliet*).

One of Shakespeare's purposes in using the Chorus is to be able to celebrate the greatness of Henry V directly; for that reason, he does not have to rely solely on the other characters to sing the king's praises. The Chorus also sets the time and place for the drama and excites the imagination of the audience. The audience, of course, must use its imagination in any type of drama, but now Shakespeare is demanding that they extend even further their imagination and create large battlefields and countries across the sea and hordes of horses charging up and down the landscape. This demand to the audience is partly an answer to the classicists who complained that Shakespeare took too many liberties with the Elizabethan stage and violated the classical sense of the unities of time and place. It is, nonetheless, effective.

Before each of the subsequent acts, Shakespeare will also use the Chorus as a device to compensate for the limitations of the stage and to continually remind the audience of a need for imaginative cooperation.

ACT I—SCENE 1

Summary

The opening scene is set in the ante-chamber of the king's palace in London. The Archbishop of Canterbury and the Bishop of Ely are discussing a bill that is still pending, one that was to be passed during King Henry IV's reign. The bill would have divested the church of more than half of its lands and wealth—in fact, it "would drink the cup and all." Because of civil strife at that time, the bill was forgotten, but now it is once again being discussed. Fortunately, King Henry V is a true lover of the church and, it is believed, can be dissuaded from supporting the bill. Canterbury describes the changes that have overtaken Prince Hal since he became King Henry V:

> Never was such a sudden scholar made;
> Never came reformation in a flood,

>With such a heady currance, scouring faults.
>
>(32-34)

While still a prince, Hal and his "unlettered, rude and shallow" companions spent their time indulging in riotous living. The wildness of his youth seemed to have left him the moment his father died:

>The breath no sooner left his father's body,
>But that his wildness, mortified in him,
>Seem'd to die too.
>
>(25-27)

Henry V is now a sober, wise and beloved king; in the same way that "The strawberry grows underneath the nettle/ And wholesome berries thrive and ripen," so did Prince Hal conceal his real worth as a youth and then emerge fully ripened into a magnificent monarch.

Canterbury then discusses how he has been trying to sway the king against the bill. He has suggested to the king that instead of taking so much from the church's holdings, the king should regain some of France's domains which would yield much more revenue. He maintains that Henry has a claim on the French crown derived from his great-grandfather, King Edward III. The Archbishop of Canterbury then explains that he and the king were earlier interrupted by the French ambassador, and that he is to meet again with the king to further explain the matter to him. He has an appointment to see the king at four o'clock and must be on his way. Ely expresses his eagerness to know the outcome of the meeting.

Commentary

For a full understanding of King Henry in *Henry V*, it is essential that one knows something about him as Prince Hal, as Shakespeare conceived of him in the earlier plays, *Henry IV, Part I*, and *Henry IV, Part II*. (See the summaries of these plays, pp. 9-13, and also the section on sixteenth-century political theory.) This background information is necessary because Shakespeare probably conceived of the series as a related group of plays leading up to presenting Henry V as England's ideal king. Certainly, the traits and qualities which are attributed to Henry are a result, in part, of what he has learned from his past life and past experience.

Scene One opens with a discussion of Henry's qualities and his past escapades, emphasizing the differences between the wild youth he once was and the wise and prudent king that he has become. The discussion between the Archbishop of Canterbury and Bishop Ely reminds the audience of the tremendous changes that have taken place in Henry since his coronation. Upon the death of Henry IV, the wild behavior of Prince Hal's past was immediately rejected and replaced by the sober duties of kingship. Thus the opening scene begins the essential theme of the play—that is, the "miraculous" transformation of a wild, impetuous, and dissolute prince into an ideal, perfect Christian monarch, yet one who is also fully aware of various, earthly political intrigues. After due praise of the new king, the churchmen bring into focus the political intrigue in terms of the bill which will deprive the church of a major portion ("the better half") of her wealth and revenues. The Archbishop's interest lies first in the preservation of both the state and the church, and thus, he must be diplomatic when he ensures that neither church nor state be deprived; he is, of course, willing to make large levies on church revenues for the sake of the state, but he also must see to it that the church retain control of her revenues. As a result, with diplomatic cunning and political intrigue, the Archbishop hopes to convince King Henry to seek additional revenues in France; to do this, he cleverly advances the theory that Henry is entitled to certain domains in France. If he is successful in this stratagem, the church will not be deprived of her revenues. The Archbishop's chances of success in persuading King Henry are enhanced by the fact that King Henry is "full of grace and fair regard," and he is also a "true lover of the holy church." Consequently, this ideal monarch, through his love of the church and through his spiritual virtue, will be manipulated into a political conflict with France. Consequently, the theme of King Henry's moral growth will be presented against a background of moral political choices and political intrigues instigated by representatives of the spiritual church.

ACT I—SCENE 2

Summary

Scene Two takes place in the "presence chamber" of the palace. The king wants to hear from the bishops concerning the rightness of his claims in France before he sees the ambassadors from France. The Archbishop of Canterbury and the Bishop of Ely enter to explain to the king his rightful claim to the French throne. But before they begin, the king warns them to tell the truth. Henry understands that a legitimate claim would mean a war with France and would cost thousands of lives. He wants more information about the "Salic law" which France is using to disprove Henry's claim. Therefore, he urges Canterbury to begin and to speak with "your conscience wash'd/ As pure as sin with baptism."

In a very long and involved speech, Canterbury explains that the king has a legitimate claim to the French crown. The Salique (Salic) laws were once applied to a small area in Germany (not even France) called Salique Land. There was, long ago, a decision made by the settlers of the area that decreed that the family's inheritance would not pass on to the women. This law "was not devised for the realm of France," for several of the kings of France obtained their right to the throne through their mothers' line. What is more, Canterbury explains, the French are simply using this law to keep Henry from the French throne.

King Henry asks if he can in good conscience make the claim. The Archbishop of Canterbury responds with a biblical quote from the Book of Numbers: "When a man dies, let the inheritance/ Descend unto the daughter." He then urges the king to fight for his claim by remembering the great exploits of his great-grandfather, Edward III, whose mother was Isabella, the daughter of Phillip IV of France.

Here, the Bishop of Ely, Exeter, and Westmoreland all implore the king to remember his noble ancestry and his regal blood. They remind the king of his courageous heritage and the unswerving loyalty of his subjects. The Archbishop of Canterbury promises him that not only his subjects, but the clergy as well, will financially support him in his fight for the French throne:

> In aid whereof we of the spiritualty
> Will raise your Highness such a mighty sum
> As never did the clergy at one time
> Bring in to any of your ancestors.

(132-35)

Henry expresses his fears for the Scottish defenses if he were to leave, recalling that every time that English kings have gone off to war, the Scots "come pouring like the tide into a breach." While Canterbury believes there is nothing to worry about, Ely and Exeter seem to agree with the king. Canterbury responds, then, using the metaphor of a bee colony in which he compares the working of a kingdom to that of a beehive: every bee has an assigned task to perform, and they all work to accomplish a common goal for the total good. Therefore, he urges Henry to divide up his forces into quarters and, with one quarter, he can conquer France and leave the other three-fourths to defend the homeland:

> If we, with thrice such powers left at home
> Cannot defend our own doors from the dog,
> Let us be worried, and our nation lose
> The name of hardiness and policy.

> (217-20)

The king seems satisfied with this suggestion and pronounces that he and his forces are going to France. He then summons the ambassadors from France. They are sent by the Dauphin (the king's son) and not by the King of France. Henry assures the ambassadors that they can speak freely and safely because "We are no tyrant, but a Christian king," and he urges them to speak frankly about what is on the Dauphin's mind.

They say that the Dauphin is aware of Henry's claim upon the French throne, but that the Dauphin believes Henry to be young and immature and worthy only of the gift which he sent with his ambassadors: tennis balls. King Henry, with dignity and clarity, responds that he will go to France to play a match that will "dazzle all the eyes of France." The tennis balls, he says, will be transformed into cannonballs, and many will "curse the Dauphin's scorn." Granting the ambassadors safe conduct, Henry bids them farewell. After their exit, he says that he hopes that he will make the "sender [the Dauphin] blush at it," and then he begins to prepare for war with France.

Commentary

In Scene One, we only heard about King Henry V; now, in Scene Two, the praise we heard is justified with Henry's appearance. Here is the ideal Christian king who has rejected the depraved companions of his youth. King Henry is seen as a prudent and conscientious ruler; that is, he has apparently already decided to wage war against France, and now he seeks from the Archbishop a public statement justifying his actions. And furthermore, he is fully and conscientiously aware of the loss of lives that this struggle will entail. To the Archbishop, he admonishes:

> Therefore take heed how you impawn our person,
> How you awake our sleeping sword of war:
> We charge you, in the name of God, take heed;
> For never two such kingdoms did contend
> Without much fall of blood. . . .
>
> (21-25)

With this speech emerges the theme which will be carried forth to the battlefield later in the play—the theme of the horrors of war and the loss of many lives which this encounter will entail and, thereby, the heavy responsibility which it places upon the *conscience* of the king who decides to wage such a war.

Consequently, the king commands the Archbishop to consult his *own* conscience before speaking and justifying such an undertaking. Here is the mature Christian king, concerned not with just matters of state, but with the conscience of the entire state (or nation) as well. The Archbishop explains the justification for Henry's actions in a speech that has to be one of the most garbled, confused, and tedious speeches in all of Shakespeare's works (in dramatic productions, this speech is usually cut and altered severely). When the Archbishop, the head of the church of England, pleads with Henry to let "the sin [be] upon my head" if there be any wrongdoing, Henry resolves to proceed; he has full assurance that he can go to war with a clear conscience.

When Henry expresses concern about an invasion from Scotland (it has happened before when the king and his army are absent from England), the Archbishop answers with the now-famous beehive comparison. This elaborate comparison of the state or human society to a beehive is a familiar Renaissance idea which supports the idea that all classes (royalty, workers, drones, and fighters) are necessary for the welfare of the perfect state.

Another facet of Henry's character is revealed during his handling of the ambassadors from France. The Dauphin has apparently heard a great deal about the wildness and immaturity of the young Prince Hal and is openly insulting to the newly reformed king. (By the Dauphin's assumptions about Henry's past life, Shakespeare also assumed that his audience was familiar with his earlier plays about Prince Hal.) But Henry is not rankled by the Dauphin's insults; instead, he responds with an evenness of temper, amazing self-control, and complete courtesy:

> We understand him well,
> How he comes o'er us with our wilder days,
> Not measuring what use we made of them.
>
> (266-68)

Henry means, as was indicated in Scene One by the Archbishop, that the "wilder days" were a part of the king's training and have been put to good use in his present knowledge of human nature.

In this scene, the Archbishop is presented as a person of great learning and one who is a master at garbling the English language in a serious manner. He is completely dedicated to England, to the king, and, last but not least, to the church. He is an admirable diplomat in the manner in which he is able to inspire and convince the king of the rightness of the engagement against France. We, however, must always keep in mind that the Archbishop's insistence upon the rightness of the claims against France are due, in part, to his desire to retain the church's revenues—with this in mind, he even promises more revenues for the war than any clergy has ever before provided.

With all the noblemen, kinsmen, and churchmen united behind the king, the first act ends with a perfect sense of unity of state and church and citizenry.

As the following genealogical chart shows, and as the confusion of the Archbishop's speech attests to, there is total and utter confusion concerning how *anyone* could make a strong, legitimate case for Henry's claim to the French throne. Henry's claim is based on a flimsy assertion that his great-great-grandmother, who was in line for the French throne, married his great-great-grandfather, Edward II of England. Yet as the chart shows, there were many in the male line of descendants who are much more entitled to claiming a legitimacy to the French throne. And aside from all other matters, King Edward III renounced forever any claim by any of the sovereigns of England to the throne of France. In conclusion, King Henry V has absolutely no claim whatsoever, and the Archbishop's speech simply obscures all these issues.

THE CLAIM OF HENRY V TO THE FRENCH THRONE

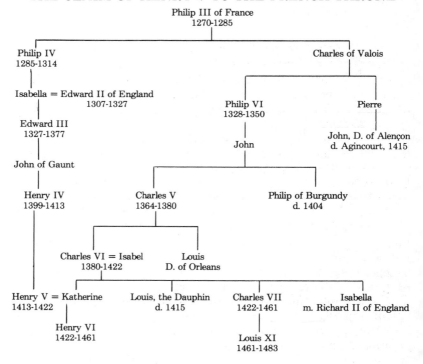

ACT II—PROLOGUE

Summary

The Chorus appears on stage again telling the audience that England has been preparing to go to war. Young men are leaving their farms and joining forces with the king; England is "like a little

like the believes.

body with a mighty heart." The French are frightened upon hearing of England's plans to wage war. The Earl of Cambridge, Lord Scroop, and Sir Thomas Grey have been paid by France to kill the king; they plan to accomplish this when the king and his forces are in Southampton, ready to sail for France. Finally, the Chorus tells the audience again to use their imaginations and suppose that they are to be transported first to Southampton and "thence to France."

Commentary

The Prologue, or the Chorus, informs the audience of the length of time which has passed since Henry's decision to invade France and the present, actual time. All of the preparations for war have been made, and enough time has elapsed for the French to learn of the plans for war and, as a counter measure, to enter into a conspiracy to have Henry assassinated.

The Chorus also reminds the audience that they must continue to use their imaginations as the scene will soon shift from London to Southampton and then to France.

ACT II—SCENE 1

Summary

This scene introduces several of Shakespeare's comic characters whom Elizabethan audiences were already familiar with from *Henry IV, Parts I* and *II*. On a street in London, Corporal Nym and Lieutenant Bardolph meet. Bardolph tells of the marriage between Pistol and Hostess Nell Quickly, a woman who had apparently once promised to marry Corporal Nym.

No sooner do Pistol and Hostess Quickly enter than Nym and Pistol draw swords and launch into a verbal match. Efforts by Bardolph and Quickly do not calm them, but a Boy enters and urges Hostess Quickly to come quickly to tend an ailing Falstaff. She exits, and Bardolph draws his sword and threatens to use it on both Nym and Pistol if they don't settle their feuding. They are hesitant, but after Bardolph threatens again, they agree to shake hands. Pistol agrees to pay Nym the eight shillings he owes him, and Pistol then says that he has a position in the army as a seller of provisions and the three of them can share in the profits.

Quickly reenters to tell the men that Falstaff is dying, and they all go off to see him, explaining on the way that the changes in the king's behavior brought about Falstaff's downfall.

Commentary

The characters introduced in this scene have no real purpose in the play. Bardolph, Pistol, and Hostess Quickly are included only because they were in the earlier *Henry IV* plays, and Shakespeare's audience would expect to see them again. Furthermore, Shakespeare lets the audience know that Sir John Falstaff—one of Shakespeare's greatest comic creations—is not totally forgotten. Yet since the king has undergone a complete transformation, these comic characters, once his old drinking cronies, will never appear in scenes in which the king appears; they have very little or nothing to do with the main story. They simply provide the comic relief from the serious plot developments, and as noted, these characters were well known and well loved by the audience. However, this scene stresses that this is *not* the world of *Henry IV*, and the mere absence of Sir John Falstaff reinforces this idea. Even the humor has changed; the quarreling between these characters is more of the snarling type and thus loses much of the gusto of the earlier plays.

In *Henry IV, Part I*, Bardolph was Falstaff's servant and held the rank of corporal. He is usually presented as having a large, flaming red nose, facial blemishes, and carbuncles on his cheeks, and as was true earlier, he is often the butt of many jokes because of his physical appearance. In *Henry IV, Part II*, he was still a corporal; Shakespeare never reveals how Bardolph received his present rank of lieutenant in this play, and critics who suggest that it could have been through Falstaff's influence miss the point that Henry's vow to be mature and responsible would not allow Falstaff to be in his presence, much less to have any influence over him. But even though Bardolph has been promoted, he is still just as much a coward as he was earlier; however, with his promotion, he has learned to conceal his cowardice better. His purpose of remaining in the army is that it provides him with a good opportunity to loot.

Pistol and Nym also provide comic relief through their worldly boasting, their blustering and swaggering, and their constant misuse of the English language. Many of their expressions are absurd, alliterative nonsense. Hostess Quickly is the same good-hearted, simple person that she was in the earlier plays. She has always had a great admiration for Sir John Falstaff, and presently she is deeply concerned over his serious illness.

ACT II—SCENE 2

Summary

Now in Southampton, Bedford (the king's brother), Exeter (the king's uncle), and Westmoreland are discussing the conspirators—Scroop, Cambridge, and Grey—who, for a price, are planning to kill the king. The king, however, is aware of the plot and those behind it.

Henry, Scroop, Cambridge, and Grey enter and begin to discuss the support and loyalty which the king has among his subjects. And as if to illustrate Henry's deserved loyalty to his goodness and wisdom, Shakespeare has Henry order a man who committed a minor offense the day before to be released from prison. Scroop, Cambridge, and Grey argue that the king must set an example and prosecute the offender to the full extent of the law, but the king argues for mercy and pardons the offender, explaining that if he punishes severely for petty crimes, how shall he punish major crimes? Henry then shows the three men some papers which prove that he knows about their plot. Cambridge, Scroop, and Grey each confess and ask him for mercy.

Henry, answering them in a moving and bitter speech, says first that these three who expressed no compassion for the minor lawbreaker deserve none now for themselves; he then speaks of the ideal of loyalty and the crime of betrayal. The treachery of Lord Scroop, who "knew'st the very bottom of my soul,/ That almost mightst have coined me into gold" and who betrayed Henry for a price, is the most incredible. Henry cannot understand why these three so-called old friends have plotted against him for nothing more than French gold. He questions how he can trust *any* man if these three whom he thought were most loyal could betray him. But compassionately he says:

> I will weep for thee;
> For this revolt of thine, methinks, is like

Another fall of man.

(140-42)

He then orders their arrest for high treason against the crown.

Exeter arrests the three, and they tell the king they are ready to die for their crimes; they ask him to forgive them, and each asserts that he is glad that their plan has been uncovered. Henry, in words that suggest his greatness as a magistrate, says that he holds no personal grudge ("Touching our person seek we no revenge"), but the safety of the nation is at hand. He therefore pronounces the sentence:

> Hear your sentence.
> You have conspired against our royal person
> Join'd with a proclaimed enemy and from his coffers
> Received the golden earnest of our death . . .
> Therefore, get you hence,
> Poor miserable wretches, to your death.
>
> (166-78)

Then, exhibiting further the qualities of mature kingship, he turns his attention immediately to matters of state and prepares for the embarkation to France.

Commentary

The treason that the Chorus speaks of in the Prologue is now discovered and resolved by King Henry in a very calm and reasoned manner. This scene emphasizes many of Henry's admirable qualities. In the first part of the scene, he shows great mercy in forgiving a person whose offense was unintentional. It is also ironic that the three traitors argue for exceedingly harsh punishment: "Let him be punished, sovereign, lest example/ Breed, by his sufferance, more of such a kind." Ironically, King Henry allows the offenders to convict themselves.

The treasonable actions of Cambridge, Grey, and Scroop emphasize the many cases of duplicity that a true king must contend with, and Henry's treatment of the conspirators is firm, just, and decisive; yet in Henry's long speech of denunciation, there is also a note of deep personal tragedy. All of these conspirators have been the recipients of special favors from the king. The treachery of Lord Scroop is the most difficult for Henry to understand since Lord Scroop knew Henry's innermost person: Lord Scroop "knewest the very bottom of my soul." Thus as Henry contemplates the contrast between appearance and reality, between the inner duplicity of the traitors and their outward show of loyalty, he is faced with not so much a political tragedy as he is faced with a *personal* tragedy. But however much the tragedy is personal, he must transcend it, and for the sake of England, he must send the traitors whom he has believed to be loyal friends to their deaths.

At the end of his speech of denunciation, he feels the betrayal so personally that he accounts for it in terms that would imply that man is sometimes simply born depraved and evil. At least Lord Scroop's betrayal is, for Henry, deep-rooted enough to be compared with the original fall of man:

> I will weep for thee;
> For this revolt of thine, methinks, is like
> Another fall of man.
>
> (140-42)

But the mark of a great king is that he must rise above personal tragedy, and thus Henry does as he tells the conspirators:

> Touching our person seek we no revenge;
> But we our kingdom's safety must so tender,
> Whose ruin you have sought, that to her laws
> We do deliver you. Get you therefore hence,
> Poor miserable wretches, to your death.
>
> (174-78)

Here, Henry sets aside his personal views and calmly sends the traitors to their deaths for the safety and welfare of the entire nation, a nation which could have been destroyed if the treachery had been successful. After dealing with the traitors, then, Henry turns his attention immediately to the duties at hand—the war with France.

Historically, both Cambridge and Lord Scroop wanted to replace Henry on the throne with Edmund Mortimer, who also had a claim to the throne and who, in the earlier *Henry IV* plays, had support from Lord Scroop's father for the throne.

ACT II—SCENE 3

Summary

In front of a tavern on a London street, Hostess Quickly tells her husband, Pistol, that she wants to accompany him to Staines on his way to Southampton. Pistol says no; they (Pistol, Bardolph, and Nym) are mourning Falstaff's death. Hostess Quickly describes for them the death of Sir John Falstaff, whom she attended until the end, and as they make ready to leave for Southampton, Pistol gives Hostess Quickly advice about running the inn. Then he kisses her, as does Bardolph, but Nym refuses. She bids them all adieu.

Commentary

The main purpose of Scene Three is to announce the death of Sir John Falstaff, and the manner of that announcement by Hostess Quickly contains as much humane feelings from these comic characters as we are to find from them in the entire play. We should remember from the earlier plays that Hostess Quickly did have a strong admiration for the marvelous fat knight. Her misused words and phrases are comically absurd, but they nevertheless possess a charm that is missing in the rest of the drama that concerns them.

Once Sir John's death is announced, Pistol expresses the common concern for greed and gain which the lower characters in this play have and their decision to join their king:

> Come, let's away. . . .
>   Yoke-fellows in arms
> Let us to France; like horse-leeches, my boys,
> To suck, to suck, the very blood to suck!
>
> (49-58)

As noted earlier, the low characters will now function mainly as looters or bloodsuckers.

ACT II—SCENE 4

Summary

In the palace of the French king, the king expresses his fear of the approaching English forces. He tells the Dauphin to prepare for war "with men of courage and with means defendant." But the Dauphin maintains that the English will be easy to defeat and that Henry is a "vain, giddy, shallow, humorous youth."

The Constable of France believes the Dauphin is mistaken and has misjudged the character of the English king. The French king agrees and urges the Dauphin to remember that "King Harry" comes from the line of Edward, the Black Prince of Wales, a fierce warrior who won the Battle of Cressy. "This is a stem/ Of that victorious stock; and let us fear/ The native mightiness and fate of him."

Exeter enters, as the ambassador from King Henry, asking the French king to give up his crown and give it to King Henry, the rightful heir; if he refuses, bloodshed and war will follow. He warns the Dauphin that his gift of tennis balls was not appreciated and that he shall have to answer to King Henry for the insult.

The French king tells Exeter that he shall have to wait until the next day for his answer.

Commentary

The basic purpose of this scene is twofold: first, to show that the French court is not prepared for war, and second, to show the disunity which is prevalent in the court. The French king, Charles VI, is not characterized as an impressive king. Even though he is correct in his appraisal of King Henry, he does not possess a commanding presence.

The Dauphin, as was indicated by his insulting gift of the tennis balls in the first act, is characterized as a rather insolent, self-opinionated young man who will function as a direct contrast to the more noble Henry. The Dauphin believes that the French should have good defenses but not because of the approach of young King Henry; he is guided not by fear but only by the general principle that one should always have good defenses.

Of more direct concern in this scene are the words of Exeter, the English ambassador; he echoes the king's determination, and he anticipates the spirit of the scenes to come in his reference to the horrors of war which can be avoided only by the French king's submission to the will of King Henry V. Exeter warns:

> . . . if you hide the crown
> Even in your hearts, there will he rake for it.
> Therefore in fierce tempest is he coming,
> In thunder and in earthquake, like a Jove,
> That, if requiring fail, he will compel.
>
> (97-101)

ACT III—PROLOGUE

Summary

The Chorus enters with a flourish and once more urges the audience to imagine the king and his troops setting sail for France and also to imagine an England emptied of all her stalwart soldiers, defended only by "grandsires, babies, and old women." The English ambassador has returned; the French king has offered his daughter, Katharine, and some minor dukedoms, but he has refused to give up his throne. Henry has rejected the offer and he now sails to France to do battle.

Commentary

As with the previous Prologues, this one serves to explain a lapsed time period, and again it reminds the audience that they must continue to use their imaginations—this time, however, the language of the Prologue is more elaborately descriptive. The king embarks on a "fleet majestical" which bears the English forces to France, and the entire "brave fleet" is adorned and lighted by dawn:

> . . . behold the threaden sails,
> Borne with the invisible and creeping wind,
> Draw the huge bottoms through the furrow'd sea,
> Breasting the lofty surge.
>
> (10-13)

ACT III—SCENE 1

Summary

This scene, consisting solely of a soliloquy by King Henry, contains many famous passages; in fact, this speech is probably the best known speech in the entire play. The scene is Harfleur, where Henry, surrounded by his troops, urges them on to one more supreme effort. Henry's speech proves that he knows his men well; speaking plainly and to the point, he appeals to their manhood, their ancestry, and their love of England:

> Follow your spirit, and upon this charge
> Cry, "God for Harry! England and Saint George!"
> (33-34)

Commentary

This speech confirms for the audience the personal and inspiring leadership of King Henry V. Even though some critics have dissected the speech and found it lacking, it is nevertheless one of the most inspiring war speeches ever uttered, and apparently it is very successful in spurring the soldiers on to make one more supreme effort. Lines 6-17 seem to suggest that in terms of the various passions of man, his spiritual emotions are directly dependent upon his physical state. In times of peace, the manly virtues are quite proper and will suffice, but in times of war, man must put aside manly virtues and become a virtual beast. It is the duty of the soldier to become a beast and his actions should be in imitation of a wild beast—the blood is to be "summoned" and the sinews are to be "stiffened."

ACT III—SCENE 2

Summary

In another part of the Harfleur field, Bardolph, apparently inspired by Henry, calls, "On, on, on, on, on! To the breach, to the breach!" But Nym and Pistol remind him that they might be killed;

they have no intention of dashing "to the breach." The Boy wishes that he were back in London. Fluellen, a Welsh officer in the English army, enters and commands them to fight. He drives them forward and leaves the Boy to reflect on the pickpocket schemes that Nym, Pistol, and Bardolph are involved in.

Fluellen reenters with another Welsh officer, Gower, who tells Fluellen to come with him, that the Duke of Gloucester wants to speak to him. Gloucester, along with the Irish Captain Macmorris, is "mining"—that is, digging tunnels under the city. Fluellen does not think highly of the captain.

Captain Macmorris and Captain Jamy, a Scotsman, enter then, and Fluellen compliments Captain Jamy on his military knowledge. Meantime, Captain Macmorris is angry that work on the mines has stopped and he will not be able to blast the walls of Harfleur with his mines. Fluellen tries to goad Macmorris into an argument, but the captain is unwilling to waste words, so Fluellen makes a remark about the Irish, a remark which Macmorris immediately resents. A fight is about to ensue when Captain Gower steps in before swords are actually drawn. A trumpet announces that a parley has been called, and Fluellen promises to resume the argument when a break in the action occurs.

Commentary

This scene, placed between Henry's charge to his armies and his confrontation with the Governor of Harfleur (and the surrender of the town), is Shakespeare's now familiar means of using a comic interlude to comment upon the serious scenes. In contrast to the nobility of Henry's inspired charge in the preceding scene ("Once more unto the breach, dear friends, once more . . ."), Bardolph repeats the charge in a bit of low, echo-like comedy: "On, on, on, on on! To the breach," thus connecting the two scenes and also showing that not all of Henry's soldiers are inspired by his valiant and heroic leadership.

The behavior of Nym, Bardolph, and Pistol is a negative counterpoint to Henry's stress on the model Englishman's patriotic virtues. These low characters would prefer to be "in an alehouse in London . . . [and] would give all . . . for a pot of ale and safety." This comic scene, however, lacks the force of the scenes in the *Henry IV* plays, where Sir John Falstaff imparted more pertinent observations about the situation. The Boy's earlier comments remind us of Falstaff, but they are, nonetheless, a poor substitute for the original.

Behind the comic aspects, however, even here Shakespeare seems to insert into these interludes something new, a deep concern about the serious waste of human lives. Nym doesn't have "a case of lives" to spare, and Pistol, in spite of his obvious cowardice and striking flamboyance, reflects: "knocks go and come; God's vassals drop and die."

When the Boy is left alone on the stage, we see another view of King Henry's inspired Englishman. In contrast to the young Boy, Bardolph is "white-livered and red-faced," Pistol has a vicious tongue but a "quiet sword," and Nym has never hurt anyone except himself—when he was drunk. Yet together, they will "steal anything and call it purchase." For the Boy, their combined "villainy goes against my weak stomach." His inexperienced and untried manhood is admirable as he deserts the three and goes off to do "some better service."

The Welsh officer Fluellen, introduced in this scene, is one of the more interesting characters in the play. While he is eager to argue and quick to show off his knowledge on almost any subject, and while he is opinionated and conceited, he is also a good soldier who shows great courage and loyalty to Henry. Ultimately, in spite of all his flaws, he will become one of the more lovable characters in the play due to his quaint and amusing ways. His antagonist in this scene, Captain Macmorris, the Irishman, is seen no more, and the long argument presented in a heavy dialect is often severely cut or omitted from many productions since it does not move the plot forward.

ACT III—SCENE 3

Summary

Scene Three opens before the gates of Harfleur, where King Henry is warning the Governor and the local citizens of the dreadful things that will happen if the city does not surrender. The king and his men are prepared to show no mercy and will reduce the town to ashes if the Governor does not surrender. The Governor replies that the Dauphin, whom he entreated to come and defend the town, sends word that his forces are not yet ready "to raise so great a siege." He therefore surrenders Harfleur to King Henry and asks for mercy. The king responds by entrusting the town to Exeter and charging him to be merciful to all the people of the city and to fortify it. He will then lead the army to Calais.

Commentary

Here, in the capitulation of Harfleur, we have the first significant surrender, and we see Henry as a victor for the first time. In this role, he is stern and undeviating in his demands that the Governor surrender the town peacefully. He depicts vividly the many horrors which could result if his demands are not met; yet, in contrast, he is willing to show great mercy if his demands are met. A new note, however, is introduced in Henry's closing speech. Winter is coming, and there is a growing sickness among the men. This problem will remain a constant concern throughout their encampment at Calais, when Henry's men will be seen as only tatters of their former selves.

In the Governor's surrender, we hear that the Dauphin refused to send help. We can assume that the Dauphin has still not taken Henry's threats seriously.

ACT III—SCENE 4

Summary

In a room of the French palace at Rouen, Katharine, the king's daughter, and Alice, the old gentlewoman, have an English lesson. Alice knows only a little English and Princess Katharine is trying to learn the language. All of the dialogue is in French except the few words (hand, nails, arm, and elbow, etc.) that she learns from Alice during the lesson.

Commentary

Katharine, the future Queen of England whom Henry will woo and become betrothed to in the final scene of the play, is here introduced as a girl of fourteen whose destiny has already been decided. The purpose of the scene is to give the audience some light-hearted relief from the battle scenes and also to show that Katharine, by her statement that "it is necessary" that she learn English, is already reconciled to the idea that she is to be Henry's queen.

In this scene, the French words and phrases that appeared in the early editions of the play were filled with errors and have been corrected by successive editors. Even though the content is trivial and hardly needs a translation, a loose translation follows:

Kath. Alice, you have been to England, and you speak the language well.

Alice. A little, my lady.

Kath. I beg you to teach me because it will be necessary that I learn it. How does one say *la main* in English?

Alice. *La main*? It is called de hand.

Kath. De hand. And *les doigts*?

Alice. *Les doigts*? O my goodness, I have forgotten *les doigts*; but I shall soon remember it. *Les doigts*? I think that they are called de fingres; yes, de fingres.

Kath. *La main*, de hand; *les doigts*, de fingres. I think that I am a good student; I have quickly learned two English words. How does one say *les ongles*?

Alice. *Les ongles*? They are called de nails.

Kath. De nails. Listen and tell me if I speak well: de hand, de fingres, and de nails.

Alice. You have spoken well, my lady; it is very good English.

Kath. Tell me the English for *le bras*.

Alice. De arm, my lady.

Kath. And *le coude*.

Alice. De elbow.

Kath. De elbow. I will now repeat all of the words that you have taught me up to now.

Alice. I think that it will be very difficult, my lady.

Kath. Excuse me, Alice; listen: de hand, de fingres, de nails, de arma, de bilbow.

Alice. De elbow, my lady.

Kath. O my goodness, I forgot. De elbow. How does one say *le col*?

44

Alice.	De nick, my lady.
Kath.	De nick. And *le menton*?
Alice.	De chin.
Kath.	De sin. *Le col*, de nick; *le menton*, de sin.
Alice.	Yes. To your honor, in truth, you pronounce the words as though you were a native English lady.
Kath.	I do not doubt it at all that I shall be able to learn it in a little more time.
Alice.	Have you yet forgotten what I have already taught you?
Kath.	No, I shall recite to you promptly: de hand, de fingres, de mails,—
Alice.	De nails, my lady.
Kath.	De nails, de arm, de ilbow.
Alice.	With your permission, de elbow.
Kath.	That is what I said; de elbow, de nick, and de sin. Now how do you say *le pied* and *la robe*?
Alice.	De foot, my lady, and de coun.
Kath.	De foot and de coun! O my Lord! These are very bad words—evil, vulgar and immodest, and not for ladies of honor to use. I would never pronounce these words before French gentlemen—not for the whole world. Foo! Le foot and le coun! Nevertheless, I am going to recite my entire lesson together one more time: de hand, de fingres, de nails, de arm, de elbow, de nick, de sin, de foot, de coun.
Alice.	Excellent, my lady!
Kath.	It is enough for this time; let's go to dinner.

ACT III—SCENE 5

Summary

In another room of the Rouen palace, the King of France is worried about the presence of King Henry and his soldiers in France. The Dauphin is upset by the ladies of the court, who are, in turn, disgusted with the lack of manliness exhibited by the French officers of the army. According to the Dauphin, their wives think that

Our mettle is bred out and they will give
Their bodies to the lust of English youth
To new-store France with bastard warriors.

(28-30)

The Duke of Bourbon and the Constable speak with disdain about England and her forces, and they note that Henry's army must be stopped quickly. The king calls on all of the French nobility to fight at once against Henry but commands the Dauphin to stay with him. The Constable remarks that such a battle between Henry's sick and hungry forces and all of the French nobility will be uneven enough to convince Henry to surrender.

The king then sends all of the French nobility to battle against Henry—with the exception of the Dauphin, whom he orders to remain with him.

Commentary

Since the English audience of Shakespeare's day would have known that the English were indeed victorious in their encounter with the French forces, this scene is therefore filled with dramatic ironies. The French are so certain of victory that they are arrogant and overconfident. Rather than being apprehensive about Henry's forces, they hold his army in contempt: "His soldiers sick and famish'd in their march . . . when he [Henry] shall see our army,/ He'll drop his heart into the sink of fear." Dramatically, the audience will take pleasure in seeing the insufferable pride of the French brought low by Henry's yeomen.

Dramatically, the Dauphin is presented as a worthy opponent of Henry, even though his father, Charles VI, is still in charge. (Historically, Charles was actually insane at this time, and the Dauphin was in charge of the royal council; this is only one of many examples of the way in which Shakespeare alters history for dramatic purposes.) The Dauphin, even though he is ashamed of the French army's fighting record is still shown here as being contemptuous of the English army; yet still, apparently, he does not take Henry seriously.

ACT III—SCENE 6

Summary

In the English camp in Picardy, Fluellen meets Gower and tells him that they have saved the bridge which they were fighting for, and he extravagantly extols the Duke of Exeter's bravery and leadership. He also mentions that Pistol fought courageously. Pistol enters then and asks Fluellen to intercede for Bardolph, who is to be hanged for stealing a pax from the church. (A pax was a small plate, usually with an engraved picture of Christ or a saint, and it was used in the communion service to hold the wafers. In Holinshed's *History*, the object was a "pyx"—the vessel used to hold the consecrated communion host and, consequently, an object of much more value and, from a mercenary viewpoint, the offense would be much greater. Thus again, Shakespeare alters history to lessen Bardolph's crime in order to allow Pistol to pun that Bardolph's death is "for a pax of little price." Actually, the intrinsic value of the object does not matter since theft from the church was punishable by death.) Fluellen refuses, saying discipline must be maintained and that he would not interfere—even for his brother. Angry, Pistol leaves, hurling insults at Fluellen. Gower tells Fluellen about Pistol's true character lest he be misled, and Fluellen pretends to understand; he promises to deal with him.

Henry and the Duke of Gloucester enter. Fluellen tells them how heroically the Duke of Exeter performed. When the King asks about the casualties, Fluellen tells him that there was only one—Bardolph is soon to be hanged for robbing a church. Henry reiterates his orders that the French populace is to be dealt with fairly; there is to be no plundering. He hopes in this way to win the people's loyalty and respect.

The French herald, Montjoy, enters and says that the French king demands that "Harry" pay for the damage which his troops have caused. Henry recognizes Montjoy's rank and admits that his English army is indeed small and tired; he would like to avoid a confrontation, but they will fight if harassed. Henry tells his brother Gloucester that God is on the side of the English army and then orders the march to the bridge.

Commentary

Historically, the events related by Fluellen refer to the fact that King Henry had to march fifty miles out of his chosen path in order to find a bridge to cross the river. They discover a suitable bridge at a place called Teroune, but the French are on the verge of destroying it when the Duke of Exeter bravely drives them back. The additional fifty-mile march was an additional hazard on King Henry's men and further weakened them.

Fluellen, as a comic character, is further developed in this scene. Comically, he is totally mistaken about Pistol and is actually a terrible judge of character. In his speech about Fortune, we see once again his propensity for trying to show off his knowledge on any subject. But, as King Henry later points out, though Fluellen "appears a little out of fashion/ There is . . . much valour in this Welshman"; particularly in his rejection of Pistol's pleas to intercede for Bardolph's life, Fluellen shows that he is a strong advocate for absolute discipline.

For students of Shakespeare, King Henry's actions are often puzzling. On the one hand, he is the exemplary, impeccable king who pronounces:

> We give express charge, that in our marches
> through the country, there be nothing compelled
> from the villages, nothing taken but paid for, [and]
> none of the French upbraided or abused in disdainful
> language; for when lenity and cruelty play for a
> kingdom, the gentler gamester is the soonest winner.
>
> (115-20)

In other words, he tells his soldiers to conduct themselves in the most respectable manner possible—even no abusive words are to be spoken. In contrast, when Fluellen casually announces that the only casualty from the encounter with the French is that Bardolph is to be executed for robbing a church, King Henry expresses no concern for, nor even recognition of, this old companion from his youthful days of tavern living. (In both of the *King Henry IV* plays, Bardolph, as noted earlier, was, along with Pistol and the late Sir John

Falstaff, the drinking companion of King Henry when he was the "madcap Prince Hal.") It is difficult for some critics to understand how King Henry can so easily forget his past relationship with Bardolph that he can send him to his death with only the cursory comment: "We would have all such offenders so cut off." The contrast between Henry's order for lenity and mercy for the captured French and the strict enforcement of discipline among the English forces appears contradictory. Furthermore, Bardolph is to be put to death for stealing a small plate from the church, and yet King Henry himself has deprived the church of large sums in order to wage his wars with the idea of taking not a small plate, but a large crown— the French crown. Thus the subplot here, involving Bardolph's theft, is also a comment on the main plot of Henry's war against France.

With the arrival of the French emissary, Montjoy, we see still another side of Henry—his concern for his men and the honesty with how he appraises his situation: "My people are with sickness much enfeebled,/ My numbers lessen'd." Shakespeare is dramatically creating a situation in which the English will have to overcome tremendous odds to be victorious—all for the glory of "Harry, England, and Saint George."

ACT III—SCENE 7

Summary

It is the night before the battle in the French camp near Agincourt. The Constable, the Duke of Orleans, Lord Rambures, and the Dauphin (who is present against his father's orders) are boasting about who has the best armor and the best horses. When the discussion turns from the wonders of the Dauphin's horse to the splendors of the others' mistresses, the Dauphin exits to ready himself for the battle. The Constable then has a discussion with the Duke of Orleans concerning the Dauphin's bravery. A messenger enters to announce that the English are camped only fifteen hundred yards away. The Constable and Orleans contend that the small English army cannot be very smart if they mean to fight them, but Rambures reminds them of the courageousness of the English. Nevertheless, the Constable and Orleans are certain that it will be an uneven battle and that by 10 o'clock they each will have captured a hundred Englishmen.

Commentary

In this scene, Shakespeare continues his satirical presentation of the French nobility by contrasting the seriousness and sobriety of the English with the superficiality and pretentiousness of the French. By doing so, Shakespeare continues to make the French appear rather ridiculous. On the night before a major battle, the French nobility join in an absurd banter concerning the value of their horses. The contrast between Henry, King of England, and the Dauphin, heir to the throne of France, is made obvious in the conversation of each man before the major battle. The Dauphin's main concern is with the beauty and perfection of his horse—a "beast for Perseus; he is pure air and fire; the dull elements of earth and water never appear in him. . . ." When the Dauphin then goes on to remind his comrades that he once wrote a sonnet to his horse, which began with the words "Wonder of nature," the Duke of Orleans sarcastically says that he has "heard a sonnet begin so to one's mistress." The Dauphin, however, is not even aware of the subtle reversal of values. Furthermore, to continue the contrast between Henry and the Dauphin, Shakespeare introduces the subject of the Dauphin's bravery; the Constable wonders if the Dauphin will stand and fight, or if he will be like a hawk who, when released, will take flight.

Throughout the scene, therefore, the French nobility reveal a rather fundamental moral carelessness which will be reflected in their resounding defeat at Agincourt. The Duke of Orleans and the other nobility speak of King Henry with utter contempt and of Henry's English soldiers as the king's "fat-brain'd followers" who, if they had any wits, must have "left their wits with their wives." In other words, Shakespeare is preparing his audience with reasons why the French nobility, outnumbering the English five to one and on horseback, are soon to be defeated by English yeoman who are "with sickness much enfeebled." The French, believing in and relying on their inherent aristocratic superiority, will go to battle incompetently prepared and will meet their deaths at the hands of English soldiers who are inspired by the noble spirit of their king and thus, by perseverence, discipline, and a belief in "Harry,

England, and Saint George" will win the battle against overwhelming odds.

ACT IV—PROLOGUE

Summary

The Chorus gives us a picture of the two opposing camps on the night before the battle; there are the whispers of the sentinels, the firelight from each camp, the neighing of the horses, the sounds of armor, some roosters crowing, and clocks striking in two nearby villages. Inside the French camp, the confident soldiers play dice while waiting anxiously for dawn; meanwhile, the English, aware of their small number and of their weakened condition, contemplate the morning's danger. The Chorus describes King Henry's walking from tent to tent talking to his soldiers ("a little touch of Harry in the night"), calling them "brothers, friends, and countrymen." He looks strong and confident, and he is a comfort to his men.

The Chorus then apologizes once again for the inadequacies of the stage and urges his audience to be ready to imagine the battle of Agincourt in their minds.

Commentary

As before, the Chorus makes another apology for the limitations of the stage and the need for imagination on the part of the audience. In conformance with the Elizabethan tradition and Shakespeare's custom, there is no absurd effort to present a battle on the stage. Throughout Shakespeare's history plays, a few soldiers represent entire armies, but here, where England's ideal king is being presented, Shakespeare resorts to using the Chorus, urging and reminding the audience that they must imagine the two opposing camps at nighttime on the eve of the crucial Battle of Agincourt.

Shakespeare continues to depict the contrasting mood of the two camps. Again, as in the last act, the Chorus informs us that the French are overconfident and high spirited, whereas the English are so dejected that the king himself must wander through the camp, offering encouragement.

In the last scene of Act III, we saw how frivolous the French were with their light-hearted talk of horses, mistresses, and love poetry. Now, Act IV will open by contrasting the situation in the English camp.

ACT IV—SCENE 1

Summary

In the English camp on the night before the battle, the king tells his brother Gloucester that he is worried about the outcome of the battle. When Sir Thomas Erpingham enters, the king, on an impulse, borrows Erpingham's cloak and is thus no longer identifiable as the king. He sends the others out to "commend [him] to the princes in our camp" and, since he wishes "no other company," he asks to be left alone to "debate" with himself.

Pistol enters and does not recognize Henry; he extols the king and asks the "young man" his name, and Henry tells him that his name is "Harry, le Roy." When Pistol discovers that he is a Welshman and knows Fluellen, he tells him that he plans to fight Fluellen. "Harry" warns him he might be defeated and Pistol becomes so incensed that he insults "Harry" with a vulgar gesture and leaves. As Henry steps aside, Fluellen and Gower enter, unaware of the king's presence. Fluellen is angry with Gower for speaking his name too loudly, afraid that the French might have overheard it. Gower maintains that "the enemy is loud" and cannot hear him; in order to end the argument, Gower promises to speak lower and they exit. The king remarks that Fluellen is odd, but that he is a good soldier.

Next, three common soldiers, John Bates, Alexander Court, and Michael Williams, enter. Henry, unrecognized, tells them he serves under Sir Thomas Erpingham. Bates asks him if he thinks that the king should be told how bleak the situation really is. Henry says no, that the king is "but a man," as they are, and if he exhibited fear, he would discourage the army. Bates personally thinks that the king would prefer to be back in London, but Henry disagrees; he believes that the king is content to be where he is. Then Bates says that the king should be ransomed to save the lives of the men in the army. Henry responds by saying that he himself would not want to leave his king alone to fight the battle because of the king's "cause being just and his quarrel honorable."

Williams is unsure of the justness of the king's claim. Bates does not think it matters; if it is unjust, the guilt is upon the king's head and they will not have to share in the blame. When Williams suggests that those who die "unprovided" (unrepentant) will be a burden upon the king's conscience, Henry responds by saying that all who go to battle should be spiritually prepared, but that the king is *not* responsible to God for their deaths.

When the discussion returns to the king's ransom, Henry says he overheard the king say it would never happen; Williams jokes that it could happen after they are all killed and they would not know the difference. After another exchange of quips, in which Henry intimates that if times were different, he might be angry at Williams, Williams takes up the idea and challenges "Harry" to a fight if they should both survive the battle. They agree to exchange gloves and wear them in their caps so they can find each other the next day. Bates calls them both fools and urges them to be friends for there are plenty of Frenchmen for them to fight.

After the three soldiers leave, Henry is left alone with his thoughts. He talks about the custom of blaming everything upon the king and concludes that a slave has a better life than a king, for he can sleep soundly at night and not worry about affairs of state.

Sir Erpingham enters and finds the king and tells him that his associates are waiting for him. He leaves, and alone once more, Henry prays to God, asking Him to fill his soldiers with courage. He also asks God not to recall the guilt of Henry's father concerning the death of Richard II because he has already made reparations and plans to do more.

Henry's brother Gloucester enters, and the king leaves with him.

Commentary

As noted above in the commentary to the Prologue, this scene serves, first, to emphasize the contrasting attitudes between the French camp—their joviality and overconfidence and superficiality—with the prevailing seriousness of the English camp. In contrast to the frivolity of the French, the entire scene in the English camp is essentially serious. Yet, there is an anticipation of great humor when the disguised king exchanges gloves with Williams and promises to meet him in a duel if they both survive today's battle; we anticipate Williams finding out that he was arguing with the very monarch for whom he is fighting.

The main purpose of this scene is to further illuminate the character of King Henry on the night before the significant and decisive Battle of Agincourt. Any time that a king wraps himself in a cloak and goes among his men incognito, talking with the common soldiers, we have a very dramatic situation. Continuing a dramatic device of the earlier *Henry* plays, the rowdy and rebellious Prince Hal had to, at first, disguise himself to become a king; now as king, he disguises himself to become a common man. Now wrapped in the obscurity of a commoner's cloak and further obscured by the darkness of night, the king is able to learn the feelings of his common soldiers, represented not by the comic Pistol (who knew the king as Prince Hal) and not by the dedicated, if peculiar, Fluellen (and Gower), but as seen in the personages of John Bates, Alexander Court (even though this character speaks only eleven words in the entire play), and Michael Williams. Even the names "John Bates" and "Williams" suggest something of the basic nature of these good English soldiers—that is, this is the stuff of which an ideal Englishman is made of and which will help Henry win military glory for England.

Most critics value this scene as proof of the greatness of Henry as a king—that is, it exhibits the simplicity and modesty, the democracy and the deep religious nature of the king. But Shakespeare no doubt hoped that his audience would be aware of some ambiguity in a situation where the king is in darkness and is in disguise, suggesting that a man's actions by day are different from his words concealed by night. In the first act, the king was ready to place the responsibility for the war on the shoulders of the Archbishop; here, when a common soldier suggests that the responsibility for the deaths of many Englishmen must rest on the conscience of the king, Henry vehemently denies this possibility. Williams maintains:

> If the cause be not good, the king himself hath a heavy reckoning to make, when all those legs and arms and heads, chopped off in a battle, shall join together at the latter day and cry all "We died at such a place . . ." it will be a black matter for the king that led them to it.
>
> (140-44)

(Yet, at the same time that Williams makes this assertion, he also fully believes that it is the duty of the subject to obey: "To disobey were against all proportion of subjection.") To answer Williams, Henry eludes taking blame by this analogy: "So, if a son that is by his father sent about merchandise do sinfully miscarry upon the sea, the imputation of his wickedness, by your rule, should be imposed upon his father that sent him. . . ." He further adds that "every subject's duty is the king's; but every subject's soul is his own." We see also that Henry believes that "the king is but a man, as I am; the violet smells to him as it doth to me . . . his ceremonies laid by, in his nakedness he appears but a man, and though his affections are higher mounted than ours, yet, when they stoop, they stoop with the like wing." In other words, the king is like the common man except that he has more concerns, and when disaster or grief strikes, one man is the same as another.

In his soliloquy, Henry expresses the suffering he endures, and he pours forth his anguish and his sense of guilt for the crown that his father usurped; particularly, we sense his sorrow when he utters a final prayer, beginning "God of battles. . . ." The sense of guilt which he feels for his father's crime against the preceding king (Richard II) is carefully scrutinized:

> Not to-day, O Lord,
> O, not to-day, think not upon the fault
> My father made in compassing the crown!
>
> (310-12)

This passage alone, given in a soliloquy, ultimately attests to the deep religious nature of Henry V.

ACT IV—SCENE 2

Summary

The scene shifts to the French camp where everyone is ready to go to battle. The sun has risen and it is time to begin. There follows a brief scene in French, loosely translated as follows:

Orl.	The sun doth gild our armour; up, my lords!
Dau.	Mount me on my horse; you, my valet, my lackey. ha!
Orl.	Oh noble spirit!

Dau.	Begone, water and earth.
Orl.	Nothing more? only air and fire.
Dau.	Heaven also, my cousin Orleans.

(This scene is a continuation or a conclusion of the last scene in Act III, when the Dauphin was discussing the merits of his horse which, according to him, possesses only fire and air; he now adds to those qualities that of heaven also.) A messenger enters and says that the English forces are also ready, and the Constable gives the call to mount up. He and the others pity the small, beleaguered English forces and hope that they have said their prayers. He has so much confidence in his superior force that he is sure that the mere appearance of his army will cause the English to "crouch down in fear and yield." A French lord, Grand-pré, enters and continues to ridicule the poor "bankrupt" and "beggar'd" condition of the Englishmen. Impatient for battle, the Constable grabs his banner and cries to his men to take the field.

Commentary

The remainder of this act reads, in part, like a pure chronicle— that is, Scene Two is set in the French camp, and then we shift to the English camp in Scene Three, and then we have a comic interlude, and then we return to the French forces on the battlefield, and then to the English forces. As noted earlier, the frivolity of the French is contrasted with the seriousness of the English. The extended insults heaped upon the English by the arrogant French officers prepare the audience to relish even more the defeat of the French forces which have shown such utter contempt for the English. The dramatic irony is that the audience knows what is going to happen, and the French forces are totally ignorant of their fate.

In the beginning of this scene, the Dauphin still speaks of his horse as being possessed of no such common elements as earth and water, but of being made of pure air and fire, the same sentiments that he expressed in his last speech. In doing so, we now realize that the night has passed and, with the dawn, the battle is about to begin, and the French are still overconfident.

ACT IV—SCENE 3

Summary

In the English camp, Gloucester, Bedford, Exeter, Westmoreland, and Salisbury discuss the battle. There are five times as many French soldiers as there are Englishmen, and the French are fresh and rested. The Earl of Salisbury bids his friends goodbye, saying they may not meet again until they meet in heaven; he then exits to do battle.

The king enters and hears Westmoreland wish for ten thousand more English troops. In answer to Westmoreland, Henry says that if God plans for them to win, there will be greater glory with no more troops than these to share the honors with. He urges anyone who does not wish to fight to leave. Today is a day set aside for the celebration of the "Feast of Saint Crispian," and all of those English soldiers who survive the battle will be honored and remembered every Saint Crispian's Day. Henry promises that all of their names shall become household words and their deeds remembered "to the ending of the world." Every Englishman who fights with him shall be his brother, and all Englishmen who do not take part in the battle will hold their manhoods cheap on Saint Crispian's Day.

The Earl of Salisbury enters and warns the king that the French are ready to charge. Henry asks Westmoreland if he still wishes for more help. Westmoreland, inspired by the king's speech, is now willing to fight the French with only the king at his side.

The French herald, Montjoy, sent from the Constable, asks King Henry to surrender now, before the slaughter begins. The king is impatient and his speech is meant more for his troops than for the French herald: Henry and his troops will either defeat the French or die. Montjoy exits, taking the king's message back to the Constable. King Henry grants his cousin, the Duke of York, the privilege of leading the troops into battle.

Commentary

The opening of this scene reestablishes for the audience the great odds against which the English are confronted. There are about sixty thousand French soldiers matched against somewhat less than twelve thousand Englishmen—five-to-one odds—and Westmoreland's wish for another ten thousand "of those men in England/ That do no work to-day" (the battle was fought on a Sunday, and the majority of Englishmen would not be working on that day) allows Henry to enter and make his famous Saint Crispian's Day speech. (The battle was fought on the day set aside to honor two fourth-century saints—Saint Crispian and Saint Crispin—and both names are used by Henry during the course of his speech.) Henry's speech contrasts strongly in its dignity and manliness with the boastful frivolity of the French nobility.

In his speech, which is a superb rhetorical vehicle for theatrical declamation, Henry is able to rouse his soldiers to a high pitch of patriotism. He would not want to share the honor of this day with other men. The fewer men there are, the greater the honor will be to those who do fight. Furthermore, if any man does not want to fight, then:

> Let him depart . . .
> We would not die in that man's company . . .
> We few, we happy few, we band of brothers;
> For he to-day that sheds his blood with me
> Shall be my brother. . . .
>
> (36/38/60-62)

Westmoreland then expresses this response to Henry's rousing speech: "Would you and I alone,/ Without more help, could fight this royal battle."

Henry is again given the opportunity to give a rousing speech when the French herald demands that Henry surrender himself for ransom. Henry reminds the envoy of the man who sold a lion's skin in advance but was subsequently killed while hunting the lion. Likewise, this very day might provide his English soldiers with new coats of lion skins.

> And my poor soldiers tell me, yet ere night
> They'll be in fresher robes, or they will pluck
> The gay new coats o'er the French soldiers' heads
> And turn them out of service.
>
> (116-19)

He assures the herald that the only ransom which the French will receive will be his bones ("joints"). On this note, the famous Battle of Agincourt begins.

ACT IV – SCENE 4

Summary

On the battlefield, Pistol enters with a captured French soldier who mistakes Pistol for a gentleman of high quality. When Pistol asks for the Frenchman's name, he hears only *"O Seigneur Dieu!"* (Oh, Lord God). Pistol mistakes the French word "Dieu" for the Frenchman's name – "Dew." Pistol then rants and raves, causing the Frenchman to say: *"O, prenez miséricorde! ayez pitié de moi!"* (Oh, take mercy on me! Have pity for me.) Again, Pistol is confused; he thinks that the word "moi" means "moy," a coin of some denomination, and he asserts that he wants at least forty "moys" or else he will cut the Frenchman's throat. After further misunderstanding, Pistol calls for the Boy to come and translate. He then finds out that the man's name is Monsieur le Fer, and Pistol makes several puns on the English words "fer," "firk," and "ferret." Pistol then tells the Boy to tell the Frenchman that he is about to cut the Frenchman's throat immediately unless he is highly paid with English crowns. The Frenchman begs for mercy and his life, saying that he is from a good family who will pay well for his ransom – at least two hundred crowns. Pistol makes more threats and finally says that that amount will abate his passion. The Boy, however, translates Pistol's speech as follows: "[Pistol] says that it is against his oath to pardon any prisoner; however, for the sake of the two hundred crowns you have promised him, he is willing to allow you your freedom and your liberty." The French prisoner then responds: "I thank him on bended knees, a thousand thanks, and I consider myself lucky to have fallen into the hands of such a courtly gentleman – one who, I believe, must be the bravest, the most valiant, and the most distinguished nobleman in England." Pistol is satisfied and exits with his prisoner. Alone, the Boy comments upon the empty bravery and the hollow courage of Pistol, who roars like some devil from an old stage play. From the Boy, we also hear about the deaths of Nym and

Bardolph, and the prediction that his own fate is precarious since only boys like himself are left to guard the equipment.

Commentary

This is the first scene we have that deals directly with the battle that is taking place. Four more scenes dealing with the battle will follow. It is ironic, therefore, that our first knowledge of this key battle comes in the form of a comic interlude—that is, if some braggart so low, incompetent, cowardly, and as rascally as Pistol can capture a French soldier, then we must assume that the French are in total disarray and that the English are initially successful. It is further ironic that one of the greatest of cringing cowards is praised so highly by the French captive and is able to extort two hundred crowns; one wonders what the other soldiers, truly brave soldiers, are accomplishing. This scene, a comic interlude, is inserted here apparently because Shakespeare wanted to further emphasize the poetic irony of the French officers' having viewed the entire battle in such a frivolous manner and their looking upon the English so derisively.

ACT IV—SCENE 5

Summary

In another part of the field, the Constable of France, the Dukes of Orleans and Bourbon, Lord Rambures, and the Dauphin realize that although they greatly outnumber the English forces, they are being defeated. There is much confusion on the battlefield, but they continue fighting, declaring their utter shame, realizing that in mere numbers, "We are enough yet living in the field/ To smother up the English."

Commentary

This short scene is the second one dealing with the battle itself. It shows that the French are indeed being dispersed in spite of their great number. As is obvious, the main intent of the scene is to show the shame of the once boastful and arrogant French as they are

being defeated by those "wretches that we played at dice for." The
entire day, then, is nothing but "shame, and eternal shame, nothing
but shame!"

ACT IV—SCENE 6

Summary

In another part of the battlefield, Henry notes that they seem to
be winning ("Well have we done, thrice valiant countrymen."), and
he asks about his kinsman, the Duke of York, whom he saw fighting
and covered with blood. Exeter repeats York's last words and tells
him in a moving speech how bravely York died. The Duke of York,
wounded and dying, stumbled upon his noble cousin, the Earl of
Suffolk, who lay dying. York took his cousin "by the beard, kissed
the gashes," and called upon Suffolk to tarry for a moment so they
could die together. Then:

> So did he turn and over Suffolk's neck
> He threw his wounded arm and kiss'd his lips;
> And so espoused to death, with blood he seal'd
> A testament of noble-ending love.
>
> (24-27)

Exeter tells how he wept like a woman at the sight, and King Henry
is about to join "with mistful eyes" when, hearing an alarm, he
realizes that the French have reinforced their armies, and he orders
his men to kill all of the French prisoners.

Commentary

First, this scene functions to announce the beginning of the
English successes. Then it shifts its emphasis to narrate the deaths
of the Duke of York, who has played only a small role in the drama,
and the death of the Earl of Suffolk, who has not even appeared in
the drama. This might seem confusing to the modern viewer, but
from our knowledge of many of Shakespeare's history plays, some
of the greatest moments are associated with a description of love
and death; added to this is the bloody gore of the battlefield. Thus,

in order to give a depth to the deaths of two who have played virtually no role in the development of the drama, this scene must be rendered within the context of a grim battle atmosphere.

Shakespeare's main purpose, here, is to show another aspect of Henry the King—one who can mourn and weep for his kinsmen and fellow soldiers fallen in battle, and then, in the next moment, put aside all sense of personal loss and sternly command the deaths of all the French prisoners in order to ensure the safety of the English soldiers. This quality of decisiveness is the stuff that all great field commanders are made of (at least Shakespeare seems to be saying this). We see evidence of the complete presence of mind and control that Henry has in the midst of a raging battle and in the throes of passion because of the deaths of his kinsmen.

For many modern readers, Henry's command to kill all the French prisoners might seem extremely cruel and barbaric or savage, but unless Henry wants to be defeated and have all of his men put to death, he must execute the prisoners before they are freed or before they revolt. In terms of historical accuracy, Henry did not reportedly issue this order until he discovered that the French had massacred all of the young boys and lackeys left in charge of the English equipment in the camp. This massacre is covered in the next scene.

ACT IV—SCENE 7

Summary

In another part of the battlefield, Fluellen and Gower discuss Henry's order to kill all the French prisoners. Gower is delighted, and Fluellen compares the king to Alexander the Great.

The king and several associates enter, along with the French herald, Montjoy, who admits the French defeat and describes the carnage of the battlefield in great detail. The king declares that this victory will be remembered as the Battle of Agincourt. Fluellen expresses his love and loyalty to the king, and Williams enters and explains to the king that he is looking for his glove in someone else's cap; he is ready to fight the rascal if only he can find him. The king mischievously hands Fluellen his glove, telling him that he took it from the French Duke of Alençon. To make sure that there is no serious trouble, Henry sends Gloucester and Warwick to watch Fluellen and Williams; he will follow to observe the fun.

Commentary

This scene is rather diverse and diffused in structure. The opening discussion by Fluellen and Gower over the senseless and unheard of slaying of the sick, the unarmed, the wounded, and, worst of all, the slaughter of the innocent young boys by the French soldiers causes Henry's men to remark upon the king's sense of justice. Both Fluellen and Gower feel that such measures are absolutely justified, and in justifying them, Fluellen compares King Henry to Alexander the Great, one of the most bloody conquerors of the ancient world. Here, however, we should remember that whereas Henry is trying to establish an imperialism, Alexander was at a loss to know what to do when there were no more lands to conquer; for that reason, the analogy to Alexander is not necessarily a flattering one.

King Henry's appearance on the stage shows his incensed rage over the massacre of the young English boys.

> I was not angry since I came to France
> Until this instant.
>
> (58-59)

His anger leads him to utter threats of harshness and inhumanity, and he threatens to kill those not yet captured if his orders are not obeyed. However, when he is assured of victory, his humility is restored in the moment when he gives full and complete credit for the victory to God:

> *Mont.* The day is yours.
> *K. Henry.* Praised be God, and not our strength, for it.
>
> (89-90)

At this point in the battle, Henry is still willing to carry on his private joke with Williams, the character he promised to do battle with if they were both alive after the day's battle. Instead, however, he gives the glove to Fluellen, a man whom he admires greatly, and then sends others to see that no real harm ensues. A director would do well, perhaps, to cut this entire scene since it does not advance the plot, does not illuminate King Henry's character too favorably, and because it basically detracts from the drama itself.

ACT IV – SCENE 8

Summary

In another part of the field, Williams and Gower enter and then Fluellen enters and tells Gower of the king's order concerning him and suggests the possibility of a promotion. At the same time, Williams recognizes his glove in Fluellen's cap and strikes him. Examining the glove in Williams's hand, he recognizes it as the match to the glove of the French Duke of Alençon which King Henry has just given to him. He therefore assumes that Williams is some sort of traitor in league with Alençon, and they are about to fight when the Earl of Warwick and the Duke of Gloucester enter and stop the fight. The king and Exeter appear also, and Henry admits his part in the charade. Williams bravely confronts the king by saying it was the king's fault since the king was in disguise. Henry orders Williams's glove to be filled with coins.

An English herald enters with the casualty reports. Ten thousand French soldiers, including an exceptionally large number of French noblemen, have been slain. The English loss is miraculously light. Henry repeatedly gives all of the credit to God and orders a mass to be said. Afterward, he says, "To England then/ Where ne'er from France arrived more happy men."

Commentary

This scene concludes the comic incident involving King Henry's encounter with the common soldier Williams before the battle when they swapped gloves and promised to fight. Many prudish critics, forgetting what a penchant for a practical joke Prince Hal formerly possessed, criticize Henry for his handling of this situation. After all, there was a *promised* rendezvous between Henry and Williams; if they both were alive after the battle, they would fight, and Williams is willing to uphold his promise, but King Henry makes light of his own promise. Those who object to Henry not living up to his word of honor have no sense of comedy, or the Renassiance, or no sense of the concepts of honor as they were understood by the Elizabethan audience. It would be completely out of character for the king to enter into combat with one of his own soldiers; furthermore, it would be treasonous for a soldier to enter into combat with the king. When the king accuses Williams of abusing the person of the king, Williams boldly defends himself before the king saying:

> Your Majesty came not like yourself; you appeared
> to me but as a common man; witness the night,
> your garments, your lowliness; and what your
> Highness suffered under that shape, I beseech
> you take it for your own fault and not mine.
>
> (53-57)

For such an honest answer, Henry awards the soldier a glove filled with crowns. Fluellen, who has just been struck by Williams, now realizes that the soldier "has mettle enough in his belly" and offers some additional money, but his offer is refused by the good, honest Williams.

When the French and English dead are numbered and the tally is brought to King Henry, consistent with his character as Shakespeare has presented it, Henry once again takes no glory for himself but, instead, he dedicates his miraculous victory to the will of God. Here, then, is the Christian king, proud of his human victory, but still humble before God as he, in a single speech, gives all credit to God, four times:

> O God! thy arm was here. . . .
>   Take it, God,
> For it is none but thine. . . .
> And be it death proclaimed through our host
> To boast of this or take the praise from God
> Which is His only. . . .
>   God fought for us.
>
> (111/116-17/119-21/125)

In this scene, we again see King Henry as a multi-dimensional man—a man among men enjoying a good jest, as a royal king receiving the miraculous news of his overwhelming victory, and as a model Christian ruler, placing his honors subservient before the might of God.

ACT V—PROLOGUE[†]

Summary

As in the other four acts, the Chorus enters and asks the audience once again to imagine certain events. After the last act, Henry left France, crossed the English Channel, and set out for London. Many of his lords tried to convince him to let "his bruised helmet and his bended sword" go before him as was the custom of the ancient Caesar upon returning victorious. Henry refused, believing that it might detract from the glory of God, to whom he attributes the victory. All of London poured out to acclaim him. The Holy Roman Emperor even came to England to try and arrange a peace, but he was unsuccessful, and now the audience must use its imagination once again and picture Henry now in France.

Commentary

For many critics, Act V is not an integral part of the drama of *King Henry V*. Many see the real intent and the true action of the play as having ended with the victory of the Battle of Agincourt and find the entire last act to be superfluous, an anticlimax to the real intent of the play. However, Shakespeare was approaching the very heights of his dramatic powers, and the act should be read for his intention and not for mere "plot."

ACT V—SCENE 1

Summary

In the English camp, Gower asks Fluellen why he is wearing a leek when the Welsh national day to do so has passed. Fluellen explains that he is looking for that "rascally, scurvy, beggarly, lousy" Pistol, who made derogatory insinuations about the Welsh people's national custom of wearing leeks to commemorate "Davy," their patron saint. Pistol enters, and Fluellen immediately begins to berate him in fierce language; he orders him to eat the leek and when Pistol refuses at first, he is roundly beaten by Fluellen until he agrees to eat it. When he falters, Fluellen spurs him on with more wallops, until Pistol has eaten the entire leek. After Fluellen leaves, Pistol says of him: "All hell shall stir for this." Gower then verbally scathes him and leaves in disgust. Alone, Pistol is dejected because he has just heard that his wife, Hostess Quickly, has died of "the French malady" (syphilis), and Pistol has no place to go—he is finished, he says, and decides to turn to a life of stealing.

Commentary

For the critics who object to the final act, one can only quote the famous eighteenth-century critic Dr. Samuel Johnson, who says of this scene: "The comic scenes of the history of Henry the Fourth and Fifth are now at an end, and all the comic personages are now dismissed. Falstaff and Mrs. Quickly are dead; Nym and Bardolph are hanged; Gadshill was lost immediately after the robbery; Poins and Peto have vanished since, one knows not how; and Pistol is now beaten into obscurity. I believe every reader regrets their departure." Seemingly, Shakespeare knew that his audience would feel suspended if he did not give an account of the last of the group, bringing to a conclusion his story of a group of the most delightful and some of the most depraved low people in all of his dramas. The final picture of Pistol makes us *not* want to see this surly braggart any more, and yet we feel some compassion toward him because of the depths to which he has fallen. He is left empty of purse and devoid of friends, contemplating a career of masquerading as a wounded veteran in order to cheat and wheedle and steal.

ACT V—SCENE 2

Summary

This scene takes place in the French palace. King Henry and his court greet the King and Queen of France, Princess Katharine, and other French nobility. The queen urges that they talk of love and not of war. The Duke of Burgundy makes a long speech about the virtues of peace, to which Henry responds that only if all his demands are met is such a peace possible. Henry appoints a group to discuss his conditions with the King of France: Exeter, Clarence, Gloucester, Warwick, and Huntingdon. The queen volunteers to go along to help with the settlement, leaving King Henry alone with Katharine and her gentlewoman, Alice.

In this love scene where Henry woos Katharine, the king's tone is gently mocking, and yet it is apparent that he is quite serious in his courting. He tells Katharine that he is an athlete and a soldier, but he is not a poet who can speak cleverly to win her love. Katharine seems hesitant, so Henry tells her that they will rule all of England and France and bear a son. When Katharine finally agrees, Henry tries to kiss her hand, which she claims is unworthy. He then tries to kiss her lips but is told that it is not the custom for maids to kiss before marriage. The king tells Katharine that they will *set* the customs—not *follow* them—and with that, he kisses her lips.

The French king and his advisors reenter. After some bantering exchanges between the Duke of Burgundy and Henry over Katharine's blushing, Henry asks if Kate shall be his wife. The acquiescence to this first demand must be met before any other aspects of the treaty can even be discussed. The French king agrees to the marriage, noting that Kate will bear sons to rule England and France. Henry seals the agreement by kissing Kate in front of all and orders preparations for the marriage to be made. Then there will be a gathering of all the other lords in order to work out the details of the treaty.

Commentary

Depending upon the mood of the reader or viewer, this love scene between Henry and Kate can either be the most charming reason for the existence of the fifth act or it can be an absurd travesty on the theme of love. One possible objection to the scene is that the conditions for the treaty between France and England depend on Henry's insistence that Kate must first be his wife. No other terms are to be even considered until it is agreed that she will be his wife, and therefore, the wooing of Kate is an artificial pretense since it is a foregone conclusion before the wooing that Kate will be Henry's wife.

Yet, for most people, this is one of the most delightful love scenes that Shakespeare ever wrote. Theater conventions demand that we forget that all sorts of political intrigues and machinations are going on; Burgundy, the French king and queen, and the English counselors are tending to the political aspects, leaving Henry on stage to expose the audience to another side of his personality. We have seen Henry as a common man moving among men, as an administrator, as a judge both merciful and strict as the occasion demanded, and we have also seen him (or heard of him) as a superb warrior. Now, we see him in a new light—as the lover who woos and sues for the hand in marriage of the lovely young Katharine, Princess of France.

Even if Henry knows that all conclusions are foregone in regard to Katharine, yet the thrill is in the lovemaking itself. He will win her to him regardless of the political affiliations, and it is to this purpose that he begins his direct and simple wooing, filled with charm and wit and good-natured teasing. He pretends that he is not the person to speak fancifully of love, and yet he wins the lady's heart with his fanciful speaking.

Henry maintains that if Katharine's love depends on his performing some physical feat, then he would quickly win her, but he cannot muster up the proper words for doing so; yet his very words do win her over. Finally, he pretends to be plain spoken, and yet he uses language and ideas that dazzle the young lady. In conclusion, the final aspect of Henry which is presented to the audience is that of the successful lover. If the theater critics and drama analysts object to the fifth act, the audience leaves the theater wholly delighted with Henry's success in love.

ACT V—EPILOGUE

Summary

The Chorus enters and ends the play, explaining that the events on the stage were mightier than could be actually portrayed. Henry and Katharine did produce a son, Henry the Sixth, whose story is told in other plays.

Commentary

The Chorus in the Epilogue simply reminds the audience once again that the stage has not been adequate for the subject matter, but then no stage could be large enough for an adequate presentation of the man who is the ideal king, the mirror of all Christian kings.

A CHARACTER SUMMATION: KING HENRY V

While *Henry V* is not Shakespeare's best play, all of the three preceding history plays—*Richard II* and *Henry IV, Parts I and II*—lead up to *Henry V* and its depiction of Henry as the idealized Christian king. Whereas the earlier plays had shown Henry as the "madcap Prince Hal," a chap who was constantly in the company of lower-class types and who was constantly in some trouble of one sort or another, yet this earlier life ultimately becomes a preparation for his kingship, and his earlier knowledge of these low types allows him to understand his common subjects and to measure his own sense of worth by their lack of noble qualities.

Each scene in *Henry V* is constructed either to illustrate some aspect of Henry V's character or to present some of the low characters as comic relief. Consequently, various scenes depict his religious nature, his mercy, pity, and compassion, his absolute sense of justice, his administrative skill, his fighting ability, his innate nobility, his ability to communicate with the common class of soldiers and people, and, in the final scene, his role as a romantic lover in the suit of Katharine's hand in marriage.

In the opening scenes, he is characterized as being troubled over the religious rightness of his claim to the French lands and the French crown. He relies heavily on the advice of the Archbishop, with the idea that his (the king's) conscience will be clear. He charges the Archbishop "in the name of God" to "religiously unfold" the means by which he can lay claim to these lands. Throughout the play, Henry V's religious nature is constantly emphasized, and after the crucial Battle of Agincourt, he is the first to give all the credit of the victory to God. At his triumphant return to London, we hear that he is frightened that too many people will praise him and not give full credit to God.

In one scene, Henry is presented in a situation where he must be a judge. First, we see him as merciful and forgiving as he releases a prisoner for a minor offense; he then turns to three conspirators and, with a sense of just majesty, he dispenses stern justice to them.

And even here, although he feels a deep personal insult because of the conspirators' plot, it is ultimately the threat to the peace of England that allows Henry to put aside personal feelings and execute the men for the sake of "the health of England."

He can, then, in the same scene turn immediately from feeling a sense of personal betrayal and instantly administer to the needs of the kingdom and the conduct of the war. In addition, during the war, he demands that the conquered French be treated with respect while, at the same time, he allows one of his boon companions of his madcap days to go to his death because he stole from a church.

Even though we never see King Henry actually fighting on the stage, we are told repeatedly of his fighting prowess and of his battered armor and sword; in other scenes, we see him as the inspirational orator and leader of men, exhorting them to rise to the great demands put upon them by the nature of the wars.

Due to his associations during his youth, Henry is also able to communicate well and naturally with the common soldiers and even, because of the carefree tenor of his youth, he still possess a penchant for a practical joke, as we see when he allows Williams and Fluellen to almost come to blows because of the gloves in their hats. Finally, as would be appropriate with the ideal king, we see Henry dressed in all his regal regalia, as the witty and urbane lover who is courting the charming princess Kate.

Therefore, in the above scene and others, many and various aspects of Henry's character are presented so as to demonstrate Shakespeare's point that here, indeed, is the ideal Christian king.

SIXTEENTH-CENTURY POLITICAL THEORY

Since the *Henry* plays are basically political ones, it is necessary to understand the political doctrine behind them if one is to do justice to Shakespeare's intentions. Elizabeth I, the fifth Tudor to rule England, had come to a throne which was in many ways insecure because of rival claims. Henry VIII, her father, had found it especially necessary to inculcate the doctrine of absolute obedience to the crown after the break with Rome in 1536. During his reign he had experienced the Pilgrimage of Grace, a rebellion in northern England, and, later, the Exeter Conspiracy, an alleged attempt to depose Henry and place a Yorkist on the throne of England. After Henry VIII's death, England endured the Western Rebellion of 1549; during Elizabeth's reign there occurred the Rebellion of 1569, as well as plots against the queen's life, notably the Babington Plot, which led to the trial, conviction, and execution of Mary, Queen of Scots. Throughout the century and beyond, England had reason to fear an invasion and the rising of native Catholics. The danger was by no means restricted to the year 1588, when Philip II of Spain sent his Armada to subdue England.

In view of such challenges to Tudor supremacy, there was a need for a political philosophy which would prevent challenges to royal authority and devastating civil war. The basic arguments were developed during the reign of Henry VIII and augmented as new crises arose during the reigns of Edward VI and Elizabeth I. It found expression in officially approved pamphlets and tracts, and also in drama and non-dramatic poetry. Especially it was emphasized in official sermons, the first group of which was introduced in the year 1549. These included strongly worded instructions on the subject of obedience. They were augmented in 1570, following the Rebellion of 1569 and the papal decree of excommunication of Queen Elizabeth I. Every Englishman was required to hear the sermons on obedience three times during the year. The gist of the doctrine was this: the ruler was God's lieutenant on earth; no subject, however exalted, had the right to actively oppose him. To do so was a sin against religion, punishable by suffering here and now and by eternal damnation after death. Even if the ruler were a tyrant, the subject had no right to oppose him; the head of state ruled with God's sufferance. In support of this doctrine, appeals were made primarily to biblical authority. Texts such as Romans 13 and Proverbs 8, as well as ones in Matthew, were cited repeatedly. John of Gaunt, Duke of Lancaster, summed up the doctrine accurately and concisely in his response to his sister-in-law, the Duchess of Gloucester, who reminded him that the reigning king, Richard II, had been responsible for the death of her husband and Gaunt's brother:

> God's is the quarrel, for God's substitute,
> His deputy anointed in His sight,
> Hath caus'd his death; the which if wrongfully,
> Let Heaven revenge; for I may never lift

> An angry arm against His minister.
> *(Richard II*, I.ii.37-41)

That Henry IV should so suffer is to be explained by the fact that he, son of John of Gaunt, did "lift an angry arm against [God's] minister." He endures rebellion; he sees the apparent waywardness of Prince Hal as part of his punishment; he is not permitted to lead a crusade against the foes of Christianity and do penance for his grievous sins. But, according to Tudor political theory, he wore the crown by God's authority; no subject had the right to oppose him. All this should make understandable the Percies' position and make unacceptable the view that Henry IV is a hypocrite.

QUESTIONS FOR REVIEW

1. Comment upon the many different attributes of Henry V that are brought out in the various scenes in the play.

2. Why is Henry so much more lenient, apparently, with the captured French than he is with the English soldiers who are caught violating his instructions?

3. How does the Chorus function? How would the play be different if it were left out completely?

4. In a famous movie version of *Henry V*, starring Sir Laurence Olivier, the Battle of Agincourt is presented with both armies costumed in a splendid array of armor and filled with pageantry. How does this presentation romanticize Shakespeare and contradict the text?

5. Comment on how Shakespeare alters historical fact for the sake of dramatic appeal.

6. How does Fluellen function in the drama? How would the drama be altered if a director omitted this role from the drama?

7. What is the dramatic appeal of the king when he is in disguise, moving among his common soldiers?

8. Analyze Shakespeare's purpose in having a common soldier, such as Williams, stand up to the king and speak his views so forthrightly.

9. How do Pistol and the Boy function in the play?

10. How can we account for the total success of the English against such overwhelming odds at the Battle of Agincourt?

SELECTED BIBLIOGRAPHY

ADAMS, J. Q. *A Life of William Shakespeare.* Boston: Houghton Mifflin Co., 1923.

ALEXANDER, PETER. *Shakespeare.* Oxford: Oxford University Press, 1964.

BERMAN, RONALD, ed. *Twentieth Century Interpretations of Henry V.* Englewood Cliffs, N. J., Prentice-Hall, Inc., 1968.

BEVINGTON, DAVID. *Shakespeare.* Arlington Heights, Ill.: A.H.M. Publications, 1978.

BRADLEY, A. C. *Shakespearean Tragedy.* London: The Macmillan Co., 1904.

FARNHAM, WILLARD. *The Medieval Heritage of Elizabethan Tragedy.* Berkeley, California: University of California Press, 1936.

GIBSON, H. N. *The Shakespeare Claimants.* New York: Barnes & Noble, Inc., 1962.

KNIGHT, G. WILSON. *The Wheel of Fire.* London: Oxford University Press, 1930.

LEAVIS, F. R. *The Common Pursuit.* Hardmonsworth, Middlesex: Penguin Books, Ltd., 1963.

74

QUINN, MICHAEL, ed. *Shakespeare: Henry V, A Casebook.* New York: The Macmillan Co., 1969.

SEWELL, ARTHUR. *Character and Society in Shakespeare.* Oxford: Clarendon Press, 1951.

SPIVACK, BERNARD. *Shakespeare and the Allegory of Evil.* New York: Columbia University Press, 1958.

STIRLING, BRENTS. *Unity in Shakespearean Tragedy: The Interplay of Theme and Character.* New York: Columbia University Press, 1956.

TRAVERSI, DEREK. *Shakespeare: From Richard II to Henry V.* Stanford: Stanford University Press, 1957.

NOTES

NOTES

NOTES

NOTES

NOTES

NOTES